CHARLES DICKENS

A PICTORIAL HISTORY OF THE WORLD'S GREATEST STORYTELLER

PHIL CARRADICE

FONTHILL

Gads Hill Place in Kent, Dickens's last home and the house where he died.

Fonthill Media Limited
www.fonthillmedia.com
office@fonthillmedia.com

First published in the United Kingdom 2014

British Library Cataloguing in Publication Data:
A catalogue record for this book is available from the British Library

ISBN 978-1-78155-278-0

Typeset in 10.5 pt on 13pt Mrs Eaves Serif Narrow
Printed and bound in England

INTRODUCTION

The story of Charles Dickens has been told many times. This re-telling of his life is different in that it uses photographs and prints to provide a visual element to his tale.

Dickens was the most visual of writers. He saw his characters in his head, acted them out as he wrote them. To him they were living people, performing there in front of him on the stage or in the movie theatre (though he would not have recognised the allusion) that was inside his head. And the places he described, they were real, too. There are many stories of family and friends alarmed by sudden shouting or laughing from his room. On investigation they found Dickens in the throes of composition. So it is appropriate that a pictorial biography should be compiled.

The pictures here are as important as the words. But it is vital that words and pictures are used together. The pictures mean little without the words and the words absolutely nothing without the accompanying photographs and prints.

This book does not attempt to be the definitive telling of the Dickens story. It is one version, one lens to look through. It is a general biography—readers must look elsewhere if they want the detailed account of Dickens and women or Dickens and crime, Dickens in America or the childhood of Dickens and so on. There are books out there that will offer exactly those options. This is, however, a good place to start reading and studying the man and his creations.

There is no doubting Dickens's ability as a writer. He was, perhaps, the greatest storyteller the world has ever seen. He called himself The Inimitable, and he was. But there is no earthly reason why genius and humanity should go together. As a person Dickens was less than perfect and that is partly what makes him such an interesting man to write and read about.

Read the book, study the illustrations, then pick up the works of the man himself. Flawed as he was, he remains a fascinating writer. Read his books, you will not be disappointed.

Phil Carradice,
St Athan, 2013

ACKNOWLEDGEMENTS

Most of the illustrations in this book come from the author's own collection. Others have been provided by Trudy Carradice, Andrew Carradice, Roger MacCallum, Philip V. Allingham and the Victorian Web Page.

Dickens and his many fictional creations, an imaginative drawing produced in the years after his death.

A BIOGRAPHICAL OVERVIEW

Arguably, all creative artists, writers in particular, owe a debt to their childhood and adolescent days. In the case of Charles Dickens this is undoubtedly and unashamedly the case. The joys and tribulations of the first eighteen years of his life, the experiences he enjoyed and endured, conspired to make him the man—and the writer—he later became.

In many instances the effect of those years was a subconscious process, something that was constantly working within his brain. But not always. It was also a wide river of memory, an ever-running and ever-present stream of emotions that he could knowingly and deliberately tap whenever he chose.

Dickens's childhood and adolescence enthralled and haunted him, in equal measure, all his life. He used those wonderful, evocative, terrifying and dangerous memories to create some of the most memorable characters in all fiction—from Oliver Twist to Little Nell, from David Copperfield to Philip Pirrip (Pip as Dickens christened him), from the Artful Dodger to Paul Dombey. The stories he wrote—the agonies of the young *David Copperfield*, the patience and fortitude of *Little Dorrit*—have their origins, their basis, in the pleasures and the pains of his childhood days.

Even when he was not writing directly about childhood or adolescence, Dickens used past experiences to inform his art. So his father's profligacy became Mr Micawber's self-destructive lifestyle; his mother's vacuous manner finds its way into the character of Mrs Nickleby; the foolishness and coquettish behaviour of Maria Beadnell, his adolescent love, emerge as the main feature of Dora, David Copperfield's first child bride—and, indeed, after he met her again in later life, in the simpering idiocy of Flora Finching.

Dickens's personality was undoubtedly strange. On the one hand he was hard-edged and driven, to the extent that very few men and women ever are; on the other he was clearly fragile and desperate for attention.

It is, admittedly, working from hindsight but it could be argued that Dickens had mental health problems—mental health issues, at least. When you look at some of the things he did and said, we are clearly dealing with a personality that was somewhat fractured. The term bi-polar was unknown in Victorian England but it could easily be applied to Dickens.

ISSUED UNDER THE AUSPICES OF THE **DICKENS CENTENARY TESTIMONIAL COMMITTEE** FOR THE PURPOSE OF RAISING A FUND FOR THE BENEFIT OF THE DESCENDANTS OF **CHARLES DICKENS**, AND, SHOULD THE PROCEEDS PERMIT, OF IN OTHER WAYS COMMEMORATING HIS MEMORY.

THE CHARLES DICKENS CENTENARY TESTIMONIAL COMMITTEE:

THE EARL OF ROSEBERY, K.G.; LORD ALVERSTONE, LORD CHIEF JUSTICE OF ENGLAND; LORD TENNYSON, PRESIDENT OF THE ROYAL LITERARY FUND; THOMAS HARDY, ESQ., CHAIRMAN OF THE AUTHORS' SOCIETY; SIR EDWARD J. POYNTER, PRESIDENT OF THE ROYAL ACADEMY; THE HON. THEODORE ROOSEVELT; LORD STRATHCONA; LORD CURZON; LORD AVEBURY; THE RT. HON. JOSEPH CHAMBERLAIN, AND UPWARDS OF A HUNDRED OTHER EMINENT LOVERS OF DICKENS.

A rare page of stamps issued by the Dickens Centenary Testimonial Committee in 1912, the centenary of the writer's birth.

He was lucky, he had an outlet for his feelings, a way of releasing pressure and tension. Others were not so fortunate. If Dickens had not discovered writing he could so easily have ended up in one of those huge mental institutions that the Victorians created—and which, incidentally, the great novelist loved to visit.

Charles Dickens never stopped learning, never ceased to engage and exploit his experiences. So the Law Courts and solicitors practices where he spent several of his early working years are essential elements in books as diverse as *The Pickwick Papers* and *Bleak House*. America finds its way, not just into his journalism but also into *Martin Chuzzelwit* and, at the end of his life, he returned to the Medway towns of childhood for *The Mystery of Edwin Drood*.

In short there has never been—and possibly never will be again—a popular and successful writer, whose art is intrinsically enmeshed so closely with his own life, as Dickens.

Charles Dickens was born in the dockyard town of Portsmouth in the same year that Napoleon was forced to retire from Moscow. Despite the Emperor's defeat, the Napoleonic Wars continued for a further three years and Dickens's father, a clerk in the Navy Pay Office, seemed to be well set in his career, even if he had already begun to display a degree of profligacy that was more than a little worrying.

John and Elizabeth Dickens originally set up home in Landport, close to the dockyard where John worked, their happy go lucky approach to life ensuring that they continued to have many friends in the town. They were popular and in great demand for dances, at parties and for things like weekend excursions to the country.

According to legend—or at least according to Elizabeth Dickens's account—the couple were at a Ball, dancing in the new Beneficial Society Hall, on the night before the birth

Where it all began, the birthplace of Dickens, Landport, Portsmouth.

of Charles, their first son. Mrs Dickens claimed that she was still on the dance floor at midnight and given her personality the claim is quite feasible. The new baby was christened Charles John Huffam Dickens, the unusual third name being in honour of Christopher Huffam, a friend and colleague of John's from Portsmouth Dockyard.

The term was unknown at the time but Charles Dickens came from what we would now call a dysfunctional family. Eventually, in his own time, he also raised and oversaw another dysfunctional family group. When you look at how he was brought up, the problems and difficulties he encountered, it is hardly surprising.

All his life Charles Dickens was a driven man. He knew what he wanted and knew how to get it. More than that, he had a compelling and blinding belief that he was always in the right. His opinion—and his opinion alone—was all that mattered and others could simply accept that fact or put up with the consequences. It is very rarely that we see him ever admitting fault or taking blame—as he once did, towards the end of his life, by admitting it was his behaviour that had driven his daughter Katey into the arms of a grossly unsuitable man.

The roots of those character traits, character traits that powered his fiction and his undoubted will to succeed, can be found in his childhood days. Charles was just five years old, happy in the love and security of his family, unaware of any financial difficulties, when his father was posted to Chatham in the year 1817. A gregarious and overly-generous man, particularly in the public houses of the town, whatever he earned, John Dickens spent it just as quickly and was invariably having to borrow from friends and creditors in order to make ends meet.

Elizabeth Dickens taught Charles to read and the future novelist quickly devoured the books in his father's small library—*Tom Jones*, *Don Quixote* and the like. Being a rather sickly child afflicted by sudden and crippling abdominal pains, he would lie in his bed or on a grassy bank as his friends played their games, enjoying the shouts of laughter but with his nose invariably pressed firmly in a book.

He particularly enjoyed the fantasy stories of *The Arabian Nights*, his love of the exotic being further fuelled by the lurid tales of his nursemaid and family servant Mary Weller whose terrifying stories about Captain Murderer and a rat that would speak, helped develop a love of the macabre that never left him. Mary Weller helped him build fantasy worlds in his head and clearly had a lot to answer for, not least her famous surname!

Between 1821 and 1822 Charles attended school, where he did well, but it was all too perfect, too good to last and all too soon clouds were gathering on the horizon of this idyllic world. In December 1822 John Dickens was transferred to London, to the huge Navy Pay Office at Somerset House. There was nothing unduly worrying in that, it was what happened next that—to the modern critic, at least—causes raised eyebrows.

Amazingly, when the family moved—and there were, by now, six children in all—the young Charles was left behind, supposedly to finish the term at school. That may well have been the case but this early abandonment of the young boy smacks of a heartlessness that was to resurface several times in later years. The effect on Charles of being suddenly left alone and helpless, as any young boy would have seen it, must have been profound.

The naivety of his parents, their blasé and, one is tempted to say, uncaring attitude, is hard to fathom. Neither John nor Elizabeth was unduly cruel but their abandonment of what even they must have realised was an impressionable and sensitive boy is nothing short of heartless.

There is no record of how Charles got on in Chatham, living as a lodger, on his own, but when the time came for him to join his family, now happily ensconced at 16 Bayham Street, Camden Town in the northern suburbs of London, Charles travelled in a coach romantically christened Timpson's Blue-Eyed Maid. Reality belied the name. The young boy was packed inside the coach, covered in damp straw for warmth, suddenly conscious that he was leaving the best part of his life behind him. As he later wrote,

> There was no other inside passenger, and I consumed my sandwiches in solitude and dreariness, and it rained hard all the way, and I thought life sloppier than I had expected to find it.

In London the abandonment continued, not physically but certainly emotionally. Charles was not enrolled at school but was left to roam the city streets. Though he revelled in the lanes and alleyways around Seven Dials and St Paul's, breathed in the foul smells of a dirty, unhygienic city and marvelled at the shops and cries of the rag and bone men and other street traders, the boy was aggrieved—and continued to feel so all his life—by the fact that he was being denied the chance to go to school and learn.

When, on 20 February 1824, John Dickens was committed to the Marshalsea Debtors' Prison, Elizabeth Dickens and the children continued to live at Gower Street, selling or pawning what they could to make ends meet. Help, of a sort, however, came when Charles was given a job at six shillings a week, with tuition during the lunch times thrown in for free, in Warrens Blacking Factory on The Strand. He began his working life two days after his twelfth birthday.

Inevitably, the young Dickens hated it. Once again he felt like he had been abandoned and betrayed by the very people who should have been protecting him. He had always had—and would retain—a clear perception of his own worth and standing. This sudden sweeping away of the values and sense of significance that were so important to his persona cut him to the core. The memory of what was clearly a traumatic experience stayed with him all his life.

The warehouse where he worked was dirty, infested by rats, and the other boys taunted him for his supposedly 'posh' ways. His only friend was Bob Fagin, who he later repaid by immortalising his name in, perhaps, his most famous book.

The lunchtime lessons never materialized and when, after the factory moved to new premises in Chandos Street, Charles and Bob Fagin were installed in the window of the shop where their skill and dexterity at covering the pots of blacking with paper labels could be appreciated by the public. The young boy's humiliation was complete.

Quite how long Dickens worked in the blacking factory is unclear. Certainly he was there for several months but the trauma was so immense that even Dickens could not remember how long his time in purgatory actually lasted.

And now came yet another abandonment. His mother and younger siblings joined John in the Marshalsea. It was standard practice at the time for the family of a debtor, who was after all just waiting for somebody to pay off his debts, something to turn up as Mr Micawber might say, to live with him in prison and this was a much better arrangement for everyone—apart from Charles. He was left out yet again, forced to live in lodgings and to survive as best he could on his six shillings a week.

Dickens will forever be associated with the stagecoach era, even though by the time he achieved fame and success, coaches were being rapidly replaced by steam trains.

Monmouth Street

The streets of London, as Dickens would have seen and experienced them—an illustration by George Cruikshank.

THE TURNKEY.

"SKETCHES BY BOZ."

The Turnkey from *Sketches by Boz*, by the artist Kyd. Dickens knew this type of man only too well, thanks to his father's insolvency and later incarceration in prison.

For an impressionable twelve year old it was a hard and damaging existence. He wandered the streets at night, fed himself on stale pastries from the 'cheap' stalls outside the confectioners' shops and lived for the weekends when he could visit his family in the Marshalsea. And in the day, of course, there was the horror of the blacking factory.

It was hardly surprising that his agonies brought on a return of his infant stomach disorder. Bob Fagin tried his best to help, packing him in straw and blacking bottles filled with hot water whenever the pain became too intense.

Bob Fagin was certainly far more solicitous than Dickens's family. Once, concerned about the physical and emotional well-being of his friend, Bob insisted on walking him home at night. Charles, desperate to avoid revealing the truth about his lifestyle, lied about his circumstances and family, got Bob to leave him at the door of a substantial house near Southwark Bridge and moved quickly on once his friend had disappeared.

Then, by the terms of his mother's will, John Dickens received a sum of 450 pounds, not a large endowment but sufficient enough to pay off his debts and leave something over.

He was released from the Marshalsea, returned to his employment at Somerset House and the family, now reunited with Charles, settled in Somers Town.

Initial joy soon turned to depression. Charles continued to work at Warrens, distraught and now feeling even more abandoned by his family—by the world, even. Nobody ever considered the feelings of the young lad and so his own version of imprisonment went on until, one day, John Dickens was attracted to a large crowd that had gathered outside the shop. He saw the humiliating sight of the boy working in the full gaze of the public and immediately ended his son's employment.

Elizabeth Dickens, angry and fearful at the loss of Charles's wage, persuaded the Blacking Warehouse manager to take him back. But John Dickens was adamant, no son of his would go on public show like this. He would not be returning to the blacking factory. Charles was overjoyed but he had found another grudge to harbour. He never forgot or forgave his mother for wanting to return him to Hell.

When further financial disaster threatened the family Charles was once more sent out to work, this time with a firm of solicitors, Ellis & Blackmore of Holborn Court, Grays Inn. This time, however, it was a far more congenial arrangement for all concerned.

Charles was content working in the law offices. He saw the iniquities of the law and its officers, storing them away for future use, but was happy to be bringing home a wage and enjoying the company of his fellow clerks. Now earning fifteen shillings a week, he was able to spend some of that money on himself, on clothes in particular. He began dressing in gaudy waistcoats and shirts, sporting a gold watch and chain, like other dandies around town.

Such fripperies gave him presence, marked him down as someone of note. Immaculate dressing was something that stayed with him all his life, almost as if he was saying

Sergt. Buzfuz.   Pickwick Papers.

Sergeant Buzfuz from *The Pickwick Papers*. Dickens consistently drew on personal experiences to create his characters and during his time working in the law he would have encountered many browbeating bullies like Buzfuz.

Dickens as a young man, enjoying the success of his early books.

to himself that if he couldn't actually be a gentleman, he would certainly dress like one.

From the early days in Chatham and Rochester he had always loved the stage. Now he was able to revive the interest. More than just attend the theatre, Dickens actually took part in some of the amateur or private theatricals that were very popular at the time. It gave him credibility and easy acclaim as he was, apparently, quite a good actor and, at one time, even considered 'taking to the boards.' He was offered an audition but a bad cold laid him low and the chance was lost. Theatre's loss was literature's gain.

The young Dickens decided to move into journalism. It took him a year but eventually he mastered the mystery of shorthand and, resigning from Ellis & Blackmore, became a freelance reporter at the college of the Doctors at Law, Doctors' Commons as it was known.

It was inevitable that when Charles Dickens fell in love he would do it with all the drive and dedication that he applied to everything. When he was just eighteen he found himself infatuated, head over heels, by a young girl, Maria Beadnell, the daughter of a banker and someone from an altogether more affluent and socially acceptable family than his own. For a while he had every reason to suppose that she had fallen under his spell.

Maria, however, knew how to play the game. She was the ultimate tease. She would flirt with the young reporter, encouraging him in his advances, but she never had any intention of marrying him. She was reserving herself for someone with far more potential and security than Charles Dickens. She drove him to the edge of madness, one minute giving him hope, crushing the life out of him with rejections the next.

The torment went on for four years before, finally, in 1833 Charles realised it was hopeless and turned his head away.

As a reporter Dickens travelled all over Britain. He wrote his reports in the back of hackney cabs or on the top of stagecoaches, shielded from the wind and rain by billowing and flapping umbrellas. It was hard, exhausting work—and Dickens loved it. For a future novelist there could not have been a better training ground.

When Dickens began to publish stories rather than journalism it was under the pen name Boz—a nickname derived from the way Charles' younger brother Augustus pronounced the name Moses. They were sketches of London life, short caricatures and pictures of the people and the streets of the capital city. They covered pawnbroker shops (a subject Dickens knew only too well), old coaching inns, parts of London like Seven Dials and even included sketches of Chatham and Rochester, loosely disguised as Mudfog and Dullsborough. They were an instant success.

Perhaps more importantly, the success of the sketches began to draw Dickens into a circle of influential writers, publishers and artists. He met William Harrison Ainsworth, the author of *Old St Paul's* and effective creator of the Dick Turpin myth, and was invited to his house to dine. There Dickens encountered, amongst others, the publisher John Macrone who quickly told him that he would like to publish his sketches in two separate volumes. When Macrone offered £150 for the first volume, Dickens readily agreed. Creditors were once again pursuing his father and this would, at least for a while, keep the wolf from the door.

Sketches by Boz was published on 7 February 1836, Dickens's twenty-fourth birthday. The reaction of critics and the public was wonderful. *The Literary Gazette* commented that the scenes and descriptions of ordinary everyday life were 'cleverly and amazingly described'. Copies flew off the bookstalls and the reading public, many of whom had already read the pieces in one or other of the journals in which they were first printed, could only sit back and wait for the second selection.

The signature of Charles Dickens, shown here on a postcard published at the end of the nineteenth century.

When Dickens decided to marry it was to the pretty Catherine Hogarth, daughter of the editor and critic George Hogarth, but this was to be no repeat of his previous love affair. He called her pet names like Wig or Mouse but any signs of obstinacy or sulkiness on her part brought an instant rebuke from the now totally confident Charles. The second half of 1835 was largely taken up with house hunting—by him, not her—the wedding being planned for the spring of 1836.

When he received an invitation from the publishers Chapman & Hall to provide the text to accompany a series of drawings by Robert Seymour about a group of London sportsmen and their adventures, Dickens accepted with alacrity. Mr Pickwick was born.

With new Boz sketches needing to be written in order to fulfil his agreement with Macrone, plus the early instalments of *Pickwick*, Dickens was inordinately busy. There was even a possibility of writing the libretto to a new opera by John Hullah. Dickens loved it and welcomed the frenetic range of activities with open arms. He was operating, now, at a whirlwind pace.

A tribute card and poem in honour of Dickens, supposedly by the Queen of Romania.

After a brief honeymoon in the Kent village of Chalk, Dickens cut short the holiday to return to his writing. The first of the twenty-monthly issues of *The Pickwick Papers* had appeared just three days before the wedding and initial sales had not been too promising. Over half the copies sent out to book sellers on a 'sale or return' basis had found their way back to the publishers. And Dickens thought he knew why.

The illustrations from Robert Seymour were far from adequate, Mr Pickwick appearing thin, anaemic and perpetually worried. Dickens was not averse to telling everyone, artist and publishers included, what he felt. The neurotic Seymour was driven to such depths of depression that, on 20 April 1836 he shot himself. The fault for his death cannot be attributed just to Dickens but the writer's attitude and comments certainly played their part.

A new artist/illustrator was found in the person of Hablot Knight Browne. Calling himself Phiz—to complement Dickens's Boz—it was an inspired choice and the two went on to work together on many occasions.

The sixth episode of *The Pickwick Papers* saw a change in the fortunes of the serial. In that episode Dickens introduced Sam Weller, a cheeky cockney boot boy from the White Heart Inn, who almost singlehandedly increased the monthly sales to 50,000. Within a few weeks 'Pickwick fever' had spread throughout the country. Soon china mugs and towels, plates and ash trays, all bearing the names and likeness of Sam Weller, Pickwick, Mr Jingle and the rest, were on sale everywhere. Dickens, of course, received none of the proceeds from this early form of merchandising.

At about this time Dickens, now only too well aware of his worth and value, bought himself out of his contract to write a book called *Gabriel Varden, The Locksmith of London* for the publisher Macrone. It was a long and complicated process, Dickens eventually buying the copyright of *Sketches by Boz* from his first publisher for an extortionate sum. It was clear that he needed a business manager, someone who could act for him.

Dickens found exactly the man he wanted in the lawyer and writer John Forster. The two became lifelong friends and Forster went on to write the first biography of the man he came to adore, both as a comrade and as a giant in the literary field.

The new, driven Dickens was now emerging. He had endured poverty as a child and had no intention of doing so again. He enjoyed the fame of being Boz but he enjoyed making money even more. He would tolerate no argument that did not fit in with his ideas, one of the reasons he often quarrelled with his various publishers and took his business elsewhere.

He knew his worth, knew that the public was demanding more mercurial works like *Pickwick*. He would give them that but he needed paying for his talent. As his fame grew and book followed successful book he became increasingly hard edged. Such an attitude did not stop with his novels—it ran over into his personal life as well.

Over the next few years, Dickens threw himself into his work. He found solace, not with Kate, as you might expect, but in the company of John Forster and other friends from the Garrick Club, men like Leigh Hunt, Hablot Browne, Thackery and the renowned actor William Macready. The relationship between Kate and Charles has always been clouded and unclear but from the early stages of their marriage he seems to have found her an uncongenial companion who preferred the home and hearth to gallivanting around the city.

As more and more children were born to the couple—Dickens clearly did not find her company in bed too uncongenial as there were ten children in all—Kate grew lethargic and corpulent. She was clumsy and this infuriated the perfectionist in Dickens. He could not order her to be as he wanted but he could find pleasures elsewhere, in the company of male friends and in flirting with the pretty girls who inevitably came his way at public dinners.

Dickens loved his children when they were young even though he did once ask the Almighty to grant him a little less fertility. He did not consider for a moment that he had anything to do with Kate's repeated pregnancies. And he certainly did not take into account the debilitating effect those repeated pregnancies and consequent post-natal depressions had on his wife.

When his children were young, Dickens lavished love and attention on them. He made up pet names for each and every one of them and was forever acting and putting on performances for their benefit. At one stage he even built a theatre in their playroom. They, in their turn, loved him although several of them later admitted that were more than a little in awe of him.

The cosseting and loving continued throughout each of their childhood days. It was as if he was trying to recreate the warmth and joy of the old Chatham period, before his father's insolvency cast such a dark shadow over his life.

When they grew to adolescence and adulthood, however, Dickens was not so easy with his children. His rigid personality and his inability to bend to the will and wishes of others meant a regular series of clashes. Rooms had to be left in pristine shape, Dickens's directions obeyed at all times and the boys in particular having to 'succeed' at whatever they attempted. They were not allowed opinions of their own. Dickens knew what was right and they had all better do as he told them. Being the son of a famous father is never easy—in the case of Dickens and his sons it was virtually impossible.

In December 1841, Dickens decided on a sabbatical and began to plan a long trip to the United States of America. Chapman and Hall agreed to pay him £150 a month until his return, on the condition that they could publish a travel book about his experiences in the USA.

In what was really a mirror image of his own earlier abandonment, in January 1842 Kate and Dickens left their children (four of them now) in the care of the actor Macready and Dickens's brother Fred and set off for America. Dickens had clearly forgotten the pain and anguish his own separation from the family had caused him in his childhood—the driven man was determined to see America, the children would have to endure the pangs of being apart, just as he had done.

To begin with Dickens was fêted and worshipped by the American public who intruded on his privacy at every moment of the day. He went to Boston and New York, met literary lions like Washington Irving and visited prisons and mental hospitals wherever he went. He journeyed down the Mississippi River on a steamboat, increasingly dismayed by the uncouth behaviour of the Americans.

And then things turned sour when he complained about the lack of a copyright agreement between Britain and the USA. The American press was outraged. How dare this upstart complain about America or any of its institutions? It was a hysterical and violent attack on Britain's greatest writer and meant that Dickens's final days in the USA were far from pleasant. Charles and Kate moved on to Canada and finally left for the return crossing. As Dickens wrote to Forster, 'Oh home—home—home—home—Home.'

Once back in England, Dickens wrote his book for Chapman & Hall, *American Notes*. It was highly critical of the American system and caused an outcry in the States. But that was nothing compared to the furore that met his next book, *The Life and Adventures of Martin Chuzzlewit*.

Sales of Dickens's new novel had been mediocre until he decided to capitalise on his recent experience and send Martin to America. Describing the new settlement of Eden (really a town called Cairo that Dickens had visited on his recent trip) he infuriated the Americans even more.

> A flat morass, bestrewn with fallen timber; a marsh on which the good growth of earth seemed to have been wrecked and cast away that from its decomposing ashes vile and ugly things might rise.

To the Americans, he was not simply describing a frontier settlement. He was writing about their very society. There was an outcry of resentment and many angry words. And of course, sales of *Chuzzlewit* rocketed.

Ever conscious of the need to save money to care for his growing brood, in the autumn of 1844 he took his family to Italy as a way of saving on living expenses. They travelled by coach—a hazardous experience—under the guidance of the courier Roche and eventually arrived in Genoa. It was here that Dickens began his next Christmas book, *The Chimes*.

The Italian trip was the start of regular foreign holidays—as befitted a man of means like Dickens—to places like Switzerland and France for the family.

Dickens had a plan to found and run a socially aware daily newspaper, a truly reforming and campaigning journal and, like all his projects, he drove it forcefully into creation. Printed by Bradbury & Evans, the first issue of the *Daily News* came out on 21 January 1846 with Dickens as editor, his father in command of the reporters.

Dickens was wrong if he thought such an enterprise could hold his interest for long. After just three weeks he resigned his editorship, leaving the reins firmly in the hands of John Forster. His restless energies needed some outlet, however, and over the next few months he and his friends threw themselves into amateur dramatics. Performing in aid of charity, the company performed two Jacobean plays, 'Every Man His Humour' and 'The Elder Brother.'

Most of Dickens's friends were involved in the project, working behind the scenes or treading the boards alongside Dickens who acted the part of Captain Bobadil in the first of the plays. There was even royal patronage when Prince Albert, the Queen's husband, attended one of the performances.

Dickens needed to be centre stage at all times and when there were no books to hold the interest of the public then acting was a more than adequate substitute. A plan to perform the 'Merry Wives of Windsor' in an attempt to raise money to restore Shakespeare's birthplace almost came to nothing when the town of Stratford Upon Avon preempted them and bought the property from under the noses of the amateur thespians. Dickens and his friends performed the play anyway. Meanwhile, Kate and his children languished, unacknowledged, at home.

All his writing life Dickens used real people as the basis of his characters. He had lampooned his mother in the character of the vapid Mrs Nickleby—she failed to recognise herself in this piece of delicious revenge. People crossed Dickens at their peril! He had always loved his father while strongly disapproving of his habits and Mr Micawber, in *David Copperfield* is, of course, John Dickens with all of that man's flowery speech and generous ways.

By now Dickens's marriage to Kate had almost reached breaking point. They were, he knew, unsuitable for each other—he could only make her unhappy and she certainly made him angry each time he looked at her. He could not say it—yet—but he was able to hint at his dissatisfaction and unhappiness in the relationship between David Copperfield and Dora in his semi-autobiographical novel *David Copperfield*.

Dickens's books were undoubtedly successful but none of them really made him the money he wanted. So much of the profit went to the publishers. And so he resolved to start a weekly periodical of his own. It was to be called *Household Words* with Dickens as editor and W. H. Wills from the *Daily News* brought in as assistant. The first edition came out on 30 March 1850.

The following year, 1851, was a momentous one. John Dickens died. He had endured a serious bowel operation, without either anaesthetic or complaint, and in the end just slipped away with a calm and a peace that belied his exuberant life. Dickens, naturally enough, was devastated. Worse was to come. Kate's ninth child, Dora Annie, died less than a year after her birth. Once again, Dickens, who loved young children, was distraught.

His pain and anguish found release in *Bleak House*, his new book for *Household Words*. It was different from anything he had previously written, comprising hard-edged social criticism of the law, in particular the Courts of Chancery, and of many other aspects of Victorian society. The fog and grime that dominate the opening chapter are both real and symbolic.

> Smoke lowering down from chimney-pots, making a soft black drizzle, with flakes of soot in it as big as full grown snowflakes—gone into mourning, one might suppose, for the death of the sun.

There is little in the book that is truly light or humorous but it is certainly powerful, containing perhaps the most dramatic and hard-hitting words Dickens ever wrote. It marked the beginning of a new phase in his literary life. No more light comedy, from now on his work would be powerful and dark, full of social realism and striking a blow for the under-privileged and poor.

In 1853 Dickens gave the first-ever public reading of his own work. It was in aid of the Birmingham and Midlands Institute and despite objections from Forster, Dickens thoroughly enjoyed the experience. The reception he received was rapturous and planted the germ of an idea in Dickens's mind—if he could do this for charity he might also do it for himself. He was restless and needed to be engaged in doing something, anything to occupy his mind and fancies. Home and family brought him little relief. His youth had gone and he felt unfulfilled.

His relationship with Kate had come to mean nothing to him and so it was, perhaps, inevitable that he would reach out for comfort and succour when and if it was offered to him. He found it in the person of the actress Ellen Ternan. She represented all the youth and innocence that Dickens craved and he fell wildly in love. All of his life Dickens, the driven man, had been an achiever. What Dickens wanted, Dickens invariably got. And now he wanted Ellen Ternan.

Dickens pursued and wooed her. Ellen was no coquette like Maria Beadnell but she knew how to play her man. She kept him at arm's length until she was ready—and then finally gave in. There is no proof but it is unlikely that Charles Dickens with his high sexual drive would not have demanded some form of repayment (although he would not have phrased it that way) for the favours he poured onto her.

To Dickens, Ellen was the epitome of youth and perfection, the qualities he felt were already beginning to slip away from him. And he knew that his time with Catherine had come to an end. His youngest son, Plorn as he was known, was just nine years old but it mattered not one jot to the infatuated Dickens.

In what was announced as a mutual agreement of separation between all parties, Mark Lemon began acting for Kate, Forster for Dickens. Kate, heartbroken and not understanding why this had happened, quietly, and with a dignified silence, moved into a house in Camden Town with her eldest son Charley as a companion. Dickens settled at his new house, Gads Hill in Kent.

New books continued to flow from his pen. He ventured for the second time (*Barnaby Rudge* had been the first) into the realms of historical fiction with a novel that has, arguably, the greatest opening and greatest closing lines ever written—but very little of substance in between. Regardless of its qualities, *A Tale of Two Cities* was a huge success with the reading public.

Public readings of his work, so long thought about, so long considered, now also became a reality. The readings were the ideal way to make the large sums of money he needed and, of course, they fuelled his incessant desire to be in the limelight, at centre stage before an adoring audience.

It took planning and foresight but in August 1858 he began a reading tour that took him all over Britain and gave him a clear profit of 3,000 guineas. He used material from his earlier books rather than the later, darker works and the public clamoured for more. Dickens, of course, loved it. Always the supreme conjurer of emotions (his own as well as others) he laughed and wept with his audience, then leapt onto a train for the next destination and performance.

For ten years, on and off, Dickens continued to tour and read, constantly adding new material to his repertoire. He could not have done it without the help of, first, Arthur Smith and then George Dolby, his tour managers, and regular use of the railway system.

An invitation to read in America took him back to the USA in 1867 for the first time since his disastrous visit there in 1842. And it was followed by more readings in Britain. Together, they brought public adulation and, finally, the financial security he had always craved. The ghosts of his childhood and the terror of failing, as his father had failed, finally slipped over the horizon

It was inevitable that all of this had been achieved only at terrible cost. He was exhausted after every reading, developed a cold that he could not shake off and was beginning to

The grave of Britain's greatest storyteller in Poets' Corner, Westminster Abbey.

display all of the symptoms of thrombosis. He survived on a largely liquid diet and after reading and performing items such as the death of Nancy from *Oliver Twist* was prostrated in his room for several hours. In the opinion of his doctors—and of his many friends—the effect of the readings was magnificent but they were, quite literally, what eventually killed him.

He continued to write. *Our Mutual Friend* was his last completed book and in it, for the first time since *Barnaby Rudge* he managed to create a realistic heroine in Bella Wilfer. The man might have been fading but his talent was certainly not.

Charles Dickens died on 9 June 1870. He had finished his last reading tour the previous spring, his doctor declaring that, if it went ahead, an event scheduled at Preston in April would most certainly kill him. Dickens's foot was so swollen he could barely pull on his boot. He could not keep his balance and his left hand shook so badly he could hardly control it. Reluctantly, Dickens agreed with the doctor and the reading was cancelled.

Back at Gads Hill, he began to plan his last—and unfinished—novel *The Mystery of Edwin Drood*. He entertained friends who came to visit, taking some American visitors to experience the opium dens in London's East End—clearly the scenes and setting for *Drood* were forming in his mind. In the early summer of 1870 he had given a few farewell readings and was even presented to Queen Victoria. But above all, as if realising he did not have much time left to him, he worked furiously at the new book, *Edwin Drood*, perhaps appropriately, returns to the setting where it all began, the Medway towns of Rochester and Chatham. Reflecting his growing friendship with Wilkie Collins (author of the first British detective novel) it is a mystery novel, a detective story in many respects. But in its raw power and superb descriptive passages it is clear that Dickens, ill as he may have been, had lost none of his power.

Whether, by his repeated touring and readings, Dickens actually brought about his own demise has often been conjectured but it is something that will never be known. His lifestyle certainly did not help matters but, then, that was Dickens, driven to the end.

As a man Dickens was certainly flawed and, to those closest to him at least, could not have been a very pleasant person to know. He was the type of man you are happy to meet at a party but with whom you are reluctant to make closer acquaintance—apart from those who loved him, of course, people like John Forster and Wilkie Collins.

Yet there is no denying his genius. Or his indefatigable energy—perhaps the two are linked. There was never anybody like him before and there probably never will be again. That, at least, makes his life, times and career worthy of study.

The birthplace of Charles Dickens, 393 Commercial Road in Landport, Portsmouth. The young child—the second baby born to John and Elizabeth Dickens—arrived on the morning of 7 February 1812. At the time the house was known as 387 Mile End Terrace and Dickens himself, when he visited Portsmouth for one of his readings, had difficulty locating the exact house of his birth, due to later road developments and number/street changes made by the Corporation. He walked up and down the road for many minutes but in the end was forced to give up the quest. The house was a fairly grand and commodious dwelling, having two parlours on the ground floor, several large bedrooms and a huge cellar. The size and nature of the building suited John and Elizabeth Dickens's view of themselves but even at this early stage of their marriage it was clear that they were over-reaching themselves.

One of the reasons Dickens failed to identify his birth-house was simple enough. He had no memory of the place as the family were forced to cut back on expenditure and when Charles was less than six months old they moved to 16 Hawke Street in Portsea. The house is shown here on the right of the picture, cramped and confined after the splendour of Commercial Road/Mile End Terrace. The Dickens family lived in this much more modest dwelling from the mid-summer of 1812 until 1814, then moved again, this time to Wish Street where they remained until John Dickens was posted back to London, to Somerset House.

John Dickens was a gregarious, happy young man whose mother and father had been in service with the MP Lord Crewe. Even after her butler-husband died, Mrs Dickens carried on working as housekeeper for Lord Crewe. Through her influence John was found a position in the Navy Pay Office, working initially at Somerset House as seventh assistant clerk—for which he earned a salary of £80 per annum. It was a varied and interesting job and on at least one occasion John was sent with despatches to the Chief Clerk of the Dockyard at Portsmouth. The Napoleonic Wars were at their height and with battleships and frigates constantly in and out of the port, the dockyard town was a hive of activity. The place immediately appealed to John. So when, in 1807, the chance of a posting to Portsmouth came up he seized it eagerly.

When Elizabeth Barrow first met John Dickens she was just nineteen years old. She was the daughter of Charles Barrow, like John, another amiable man (who was later charged with embezzlement and, as a consequence, had to flee abroad) and a senior member of staff in the Portsmouth Pay Office, in effect John's departmental head. Barrow was pleased to encourage John Dickens's suite—the young man was personable and, in outward appearances at least, the ideal match for his daughter. In fact, it was a disaster waiting to happen. Elizabeth was as reckless and self-indulgent as her future husband. She loved parties and dances, thoroughly enjoyed entertaining, and had a silly girlish charm that is acceptable in the very young but which does not make for a secure and solid marriage.

John Dickens
to Elizabeth Barrow

A facsimile of the signatures of John Dickens and Elizabeth Barrow in the church register of St Mary le Strand where they were married in 1809. John was twenty-three years old at the time and already the qualities that were to haunt him and his family all his life were quite evident. Like Mr Micawber in *David Copperfield*, the character his son clearly based on John, he had an interesting, even attractive personality and was always given to the flamboyant and grand gesture. He loved good company and would hold an audience spellbound with his stories and anecdotes—although there is no evidence that he drank particularly heavily. Yet, with hindsight, it is hard to like him. As with Micawber he was a self-absorbed individual who totally failed to adapt or even care for his family—apart from a few well-placed aphorisms and remarks.

After being posted back to Somerset House from Portsmouth, there was a three-year stay in London for John. Then he was sent to work in the Medway dockyard at Chatham. It was the winter of 1817 and John Dickens found what he considered the perfect home for his family, 2 Ordnance Terrace. The number was later changed to 11 but there was never any confusion about this home in the young Charles's memory. He loved his time in Chatham and considered it the most perfect childhood a person could ever have. It was hardly surprising as the house sat at the top of a slope with views away to the Medway in the distance. Nearby there was a huge cornfield to explore and romp in. By now there were five children in the Dickens household and Charles was more than happy to be hoisted onto a tabletop—in the house or in one of the town's many alehouses—to perform one party piece after another. He fell in love with the girl next door and relished being involved in the never-ending round of parties, magic lantern shows and trips down river on board the Admiralty yacht— something of a 'perk of the job' for John and his family.

11, ORDNANCE TERRACE, CHATHAM. (888) *where Charles Dickens lived from 1817 to 1821*

By 1821, however, John Dickens could no longer afford the rent on 2 Ordnance Terrace. To be fair to him, it was not all John's fault. The Navy Board insisted on paying its salaried staff on a three-monthly basis and, with John and Elizabeth never being the most frugal of people, by the time pay day arrived they were having to live on credit—which would have been fine if they had then paid off their debts. They didn't and so the amount of the debt simply increased month by month. John Dickens's solution to the problem was to move to a smaller house, 18 St Mary's Place, the Brook, Chatham. Despite the straitened circumstance, young Charles continued to enjoy his time in Chatham. He did well at the school next door, run by the Revd William Giles, and his particular pleasure was to lie out in the fields, reading, as his friends played about him.

From an early age, Charles Dickens loved the theatre, happily losing himself in the glory of the costumes and the intricate plots that were all the rage at the time. Elizabeth Dickens's sister Fanny had recently married an army surgeon called Dr Lamert and, with him and his stepson James, Charles began to attend The Theatre Royal in Rochester. It was a small enough place but here Dickens first saw renowned actors like Edmund Keane and Charles Matthews and, a particular favourite, the great clown Joey Grimaldi. Dr Lamert even organised private theatricals and so, for the first time, Charles was able to get a glimpse behind the scenes. It was an experience that would later stand him in good stead.

The Mitre Inn, Chatham, one of several public houses frequented by John Dickens. John probably preferred the comradeship and camaraderie of the pub to imbibing too much but he and the landlord, John Tribe, certainly knew each other very well. It was here that the boy Charles gave the first of his public performances, a famous place to make his 'stage' debut. The inn was renowned for the quality of its lodging, its food and drink, Lord Nelson having stayed there and also King William IV when he was still the Duke of Clarence.

The Navy Pay Office in the dockyard at Chatham. John Dickens worked here for six years and the young Charles was a regular visitor to the establishment, calling in to see him and waiting for his father at the end of the working day. Time spent in a 'counting house' like this could not have been conducive to a mercurial and fun-loving man like John—small wonder he lived for the end of the day when he could escape the confines of the Pay Office to the bonhomie of the local inns and public houses.

In December 1822 John Dickens was once more transferred to London, to work again at Somerset House. At this distance it is hard to know if the posting was because he was good at his job or because, with his finances running out of control, the Navy Board did not want an embarrassment on their hands. Whatever the reasons, John Dickens had to pay off his creditors before he could leave Chatham and the only way he could do this was by selling many of the family's prized possessions, including the small library that Charles loved so much. The family moved but Charles stayed behind, supposedly to finish off the term in school. When the time came for him to rejoin his family he was packed into a stagecoach, muffled up by straw. And so he bade farewell to Chatham and Kent and to an idyllic period of time.

Charles Dickens fully expected to continue his schooling in London. After all, his sister Fanny, a gifted musician, had recently won a scholarship to the Royal Academy of Music and was now boarding away from home. John Dickens still had to pay towards her upkeep, however, and there was simply not enough money to cater for Charles as well. And so the young boy became a wanderer, roaming through the streets of London, running messages for his father and observing the teeming masses, poor and rich alike, who thronged the city. He would not have recognised it as such but this was far more of an education for the future novelist than a whole world of classroom desks. He quickly came to know the slums of the East End and the maze of alleyways and lanes that proliferated in old London—and in his own way he fell in love with them. But at the time it was not what he wanted and he resented the inability of his parents to provide him with the formal education he felt he was due.

John Dickens may have moved jobs and location but he did not change his profligate ways. There was real poverty in the house at Bayham Street and Charles was often despatched to the nearest pawn shop to add at least something to the family finances by 'hocking' clothes, books and jewellery. It brought in some money but it was never enough and the family was soon in debt to local tradesmen. They moved to smaller quarters in Gower Street where Elizabeth Dickens's sole contribution to the economy of the home was to pay for and put up a brass plate advertising 'Mrs Dickens's Establishment for Girls.' Charles was sent around the area with leaflets, advertising the proposed school, but no-one ever enrolled and all that came out of the enterprise was a deeper pool of debt.

It was inevitable that, sooner or later, John Dickens's creditors would run out of patience. In February 1824 he was arrested for a debt of some £40 or £50 and sent to the Marshalsea Prison, the remains of which are shown here. John might well have regaled his son with the advice Charles would later put into the mouth of Mr Micawber—'Annual income twenty pounds, annual expenditure nineteen and six, result happiness. Annual income twenty pounds, annual expenditure twenty pounds and six, result misery'—but conditions inside the Marshalsea were quite to John's liking. As an educated man he quickly achieved a degree of status with the other prisoners and lived a fairly comfortable life. Elizabeth and his family joined him in the prison—all except Charles.

James Lamert, from the Chatham days, now in London as the manager of Warren's Blacking Factory at Number 30, The Strand, offered Charles a job at the princely sum of six shillings a week. The boy began working in the dilapidated and rat infested old warehouse overlooking the Thames (on the left in this print) when he was just twelve years old. To Charles it felt like the end of the world. He was being relegated to the ranks of the working classes and had lost, as he later wrote, the opportunity of ever becoming 'a learned and distinguished man.' He was found lodgings and was left to fend for himself on his six pence a week. It was an amazing decision by John and Elizabeth, yet another example of the young man being abandoned by his family.

A rather romanticised illustration from *David Copperfield*, this nevertheless shows what life would have been like for Dickens, left to wander the streets and feed himself as best he could while the rest of the family resided in relative comfort inside the Marshalsea. It was perhaps inevitable that his childhood affliction of abdominal pains should return and, at last, even his thoughtless father was concerned enough to change his son's lodgings, closer to the prison so that he would be able to visit in the evenings and at weekends.

John Dickens's incarceration did not last long. In April 1824 a small gratuity from his mother's estate enabled him to pay off his creditors and return to work at Somerset House. The family moved to a house in Johnson Street in Somers Town—a squalid enough place, shown here in later days after it had become The David Copperfield Library for Children. Charles was overjoyed at his father's release but then quickly dismayed to find that there was to be no reprieve for him—he would continue to work in the Blacking Factory. It was only after a quarrel between John Dickens and John Lamert that Charles was removed from the factory—and even then his mother, anxious not to lose the income of six valuable shillings a week, was desperate to send him back. In perhaps the best thing his father ever did for him, John Dickens refused to allow it, his son would not return to the factory.

In the summer of 1824 Charles Dickens finally went back to school. He was enrolled at Wellington House Academy in Hampstead Road. He spent three years at this chaotic and liberal establishment, run by Mr William Jones, a Welshman whose sole contribution to the education of his pupils seems to have been in drawing straight lines in their exercise books and administering beatings to those he felt required them. Nevertheless, Dickens enjoyed his time there and did actually learn some Latin and mathematics. He and his classmates kept pet mice in their desks, he wrote and performed little plays and stories for his friends' amusement and there is even a possibility that he became the equivalent of Head Boy.

STEERFORTH AND MR MELL. — DAVID COPPERFIELD.

The staff at Wellington House were fortunately, far better qualified and experienced than Mr Jones. A man by the name of Taylor taught writing and reading and to him we owe at least some credit for developing the Dickens style. The school, located in a wooden shack behind the substantial front building where Jones lived, was not unlike Dr Strong's establishment in *David Copperfield*. Dickens may not have liked the school but he enjoyed his spare and social time with the other boys. It was certainly a lot better than the Blacking Factory.

Walking to school each day, Dickens continued to observe London life, the fights and squabbles of the people lining the streets and the rich variety of characters he saw before him. Still John Dickens did not curb his spendthrift ways and in March 1827 the family were evicted from Johnson Street for non-payment of rent. They moved to 17 The Polygon, a run-down area of Somers Town. With no money to pay her fees, Fanny was forced to leave the Royal Academy and Charles was removed from Wellington House. His school days were over.

Charles Dickens went to work, first, in the office of Mr Molloy, a solicitor, before joining the firm of Ellis & Blackmore, Solicitors, of Gray's Inn. Debt continued to plague his family but Charles, although really little more than an office boy, was finally earning a reasonable salary. Dressing, now, in flamboyant waistcoats and adorning himself with golden watch chains and rings, he began to frequent the theatre once more—something he had not done since his childhood days in Chatham. He and his friends from the law firm would treat themselves to a meal before the performance and then buy cheap tickets in the gallery for the second half of the show. He even took part in 'private theatricals,' happily performing in front of friends, acquaintances and the paying public.

Having somehow persuaded the Navy Board to retire him on a substantial pension, John Dickens began work as a shorthand reporter in the Gallery of the House of Commons where he quickly became renowned for the quality and accuracy of his reporting. Charles, tiring of the law, decided to follow in his father's footsteps but there were no vacancies and, despite having taught himself the intricate art of shorthand, he was forced to spend two years as a freelance reporter at Doctors' Commons (shown here) where five different courts sat in judgement. It was excellent training for the young man whose skill at shorthand and the reproduction of speeches soon came to equal that of his father.

During this time Charles fell madly in love with a girl just a year older than him, Maria Beadnell. Dickens thought his feelings were reciprocated but she was the flirtatious daughter of a banker, well set in the world, and clearly had no intention of marrying anyone without either money or prospects. Dickens endured the agony of unrequited love for three years before, in 1833, he finally realised that the case was a hopeless one. It was a cruel episode but the affair taught him a lesson that would stay with him all his life—never again would he allow himself to be ruled as Maria had ruled him.

Romance aside, by now Charles Dickens's big chance had come. In 1832 John Barrow, brother-in-law of John Dickens, employed his young nephew as a fully fledged parliamentary reporter on *Mirror of Parliament*. This was the age of electoral reform in Britain and feelings were running high as the great Reform Bill, radically altering the nature of Parliament and the whole franchise situation, was driven through the Commons. All across the country enormous meetings or gatherings of interested parties were held, many of them ending in fights and near-riots as the Tory supporters of the Duke of Wellington clashed with the more radical Whigs. Never before (or since) had politics so consumed the nation. It was an age of anger and tense excitement.

Dickens, already renowned because of his reporting and journalism, saw it all. He was in constant demand, being summoned to Norfolk one day, Bath the next, Portsmouth the day after that. He travelled between one meeting and the next, snatching his meals where and when he could, covering the whole country by stagecoach and carriage. Within a few months he knew all the old coaching inns, sleeping in their flea-ridden beds. He was familiar with the innkeepers and boot boys, the local dignitaries and journalists—and loved every minute of it. Like everything he did in his life, Dickens threw himself headlong into the role of reporter and did it all at frenetic pace. The fascination he discovered in travel and wayside inns found its way into books like *Pickwick Papers* and created what is still thought of as Dickens's England.

Dickens posting by hand his first story manuscript to the editor of a small periodical called the *Monthly Magazine*. He had ambitions beyond being a mere journalist; story writing was what he really wanted to do. As he himself later wrote this first effort was 'dropped stealthily one evening at twilight, with fear and trembling, into a dark letter box in a dark office, up a dark court in Fleet Street.' The story was called 'A Dinner at Poplar Walk' and, to his relief, the editor accepted it—and asked for more. His first few stories were published anonymously and only after the first half dozen did the pseudonym Boz begin to appear attached to the articles.

Furnival's Inn where Dickens was living when the first of his 'Sketches' were published, having moved out of his parents' house a few months before. The sketches were an immediate success and soon Dickens was being lionised by the literary establishment. Invitations to dine came flooding in. George Hogarth, the editor of the *Evening Chronicle* commissioned more articles and asked Dickens to dinner at his house just off the Fulham Road. There he met Hogarth's eldest daughter Catherine, a pretty but compliant girl who, like the other Hogarth girls, quickly fell under the Dickens spell.

Catherine Hogarth at about the time she and Dickens met. From the beginning of their relationship, Dickens was in total control and was determined to have her behave exactly as he wanted. He called her pet names but also regularly wrote to her, complaining or telling her off for silly comments or childish and thoughtless behaviour. She had a tendency to sulk or pout and the new, hard-edged Dickens would have none of it. Catherine—Kate as he called her—was compliant and accepted it as the way things were.

St Luke's Church in Chelsea where Dickens and Kate were married in April 1836. By now the success of the 'Sketches,' published in book form as well as monthly parts, had made him financially secure enough to risk marriage—even though he had recently been forced to borrow money from a friend by the name of Thomas Mitton to stave off another financial disaster for his still improvident father. He was confident in his ability, in particular his ability to earn money—not for him the iniquities of the sponging house and the debtors' prison.

The frontispiece of *Sketches by Boz*, Dickens's first book. The illustration is by George Cruikshank and shows writer and artist ascending in a hot air balloon—to the rapturous applause of the public. Balloons, like Dickens's fiction, were still unique enough to cause incredible interest in the public. Dickens's name was, as yet, unknown but the pseudonym Boz was spoken about with growing awe and interest.

London as Dickens would have known it, a painting by the marine artist W. L. Wylie, showing the dome of St Paul's in the background. This was the part of London that Dickens knew well, having spent many hours roaming the narrow streets around the cathedral and poking about in the tiny shops that lined the alleyways.

Dickens's 'Sketches' were humorous but inevitably tinged with social concern. He had seen and endured poverty himself and knew the evils that things like drink could bring to people. This Cruikshank illustration shows 'The Gin Shop'—gin was cheap and readily available and there was no wonder that people turned to alcohol in order to forget the rigours of life in a state that offered no help or assistance to anyone in trouble.

Dickens's name will forever be associated with the stagecoach era. In the early part of the nineteenth century a wide network of coach routes spread like spiders webs across the country and during his time as a reporter Dickens regularly used them to get from one meeting to the next. This view shows him arriving at The Kings Head, later fictionalised as The Maypole in *Barnaby Rudge*. It is a romantic version of travel and the times but by the late 1830s stagecoaches were already being superseded by railways and soon the only vehicles powered by horses were the London omnibuses.

To the publishers Chapman & Hall must go the credit for bringing *The Pickwick Papers* to the attention of the world. It was their idea to use Dickens to supply the text for the amusing and mock-heroic sketches of the artist Robert Seymour. Dickens readily agreed to the proposal, recognising William Hall as the very man who had sold him a copy of *The Monthly Magazine*, containing his first printed story—it was, Dickens felt, an omen. Dickens would play 'second fiddle' to no-one, however. He may have accepted Chapman and Hall's offer but, right from the beginning, he was clear that the text should drive the illustrations, not the other way around. Mr Pickwick with his tights and gaiters may have 'inspired involuntary awe and respect' in the members of the Pickwick Club but in the eyes of the public—after an initial hiccup—he only added greatly to the fame and success of the young writer.

Dickens and the depressive, mentally unbalanced Seymour did not see eye to eye, either about the way the story was progressing or the way that Pickwick looked in the pictures. So critical was Dickens about the illustrations that Seymour was plunged into a terminal bout of depression which only ended when he took his own life. Dickens was unconcerned—his serial story was far more important. To begin with sales of the monthly parts were not encouraging and Chapman & Hall even considered ending publication. But Dickens knew the power of his creation and was insistent that Pickwick should continue. The first problem to be overcome was to find a new illustrator. Several were tried before, eventually, a young and unknown artist by the name of Hablot Knight Browne was appointed. Calling himself Phiz—to match with Boz—Browne was an inspired choice, one which nobody, not least Dickens, ever regretted.

The real turning point for Pickwick came in the sixth issue when Dickens hit on the character of the Cockney boot boy Sam Weller. The public immediately fell in love with his wit and approach to life—although these days much of his humour and funny asides seem too forced and hollow. Dickens drew on Cockney idioms and speech patterns for Sam and people at the time recognised him for what he was—one of them! This drawing by Phiz shows the first meeting of Sam and Mr Pickwick in the yard of the White Hart Inn.

The frontispiece of *The Pickwick Papers*. Within weeks of the appearance of Sam Weller, the success of the new publishing enterprise was assured, almost 50,000 copies being sold each month. These were amazing sales figures and an incredible turn around in fortunes. Dickens's future as a writer of popular fiction was assured. Pickwick-mania seized the land and Dickens basked in the glow of success and financial security.

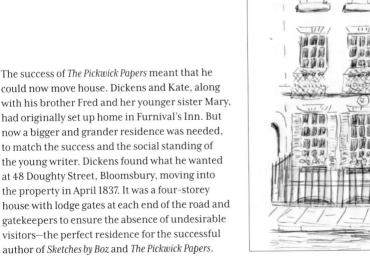

The success of *The Pickwick Papers* meant that he could now move house. Dickens and Kate, along with his brother Fred and her younger sister Mary, had originally set up home in Furnival's Inn. But now a bigger and grander residence was needed, to match the success and the social standing of the young writer. Dickens found what he wanted at 48 Doughty Street, Bloomsbury, moving into the property in April 1837. It was a four-storey house with lodge gates at each end of the road and gatekeepers to ensure the absence of undesirable visitors—the perfect residence for the successful author of *Sketches by Boz* and *The Pickwick Papers*.

The sudden and unexpected death of seventeen-year-old Mary Hogarth on 7 May 1837, soon after the family had moved into Doughty Street, devastated Dickens. He was distraught, couldn't write and, many thought, was in danger of losing his mind. Quite why the death should affect him so badly is hard to define, as is Kate's response to her husband's obvious distress. Just what did he feel for her? Had he married the wrong Hogarth daughter? Whatever the reason, he was never able to forget her and virtually all his future female characters were idealised versions of Mary.

Dickens had always admired the great clown Joey Grimaldi, ever since he had first seen him perform in Rochester. So when the opportunity came to edit his memoirs, Dickens immediately agreed, despite having to produce regular serialised pages for *Pickwick* at the same time. The book was hardly a success, at least not in the way his fiction was a success, but it was something Dickens felt he had to do, to pay homage to the great man.

Mile End Cottage near Exeter. This was the place to which John and Elizabeth Dickens were exiled when, in March 1839, Charles grew tired of his father's debts—and of him obtaining credit on the strength of his son's famous name. It was rural and solitary, hardly the place to appeal to the gregarious John, but Dickens believed that it was exactly the right environment to keep his father out of mischief. As might be expected, John and Elizabeth did not stay there long.

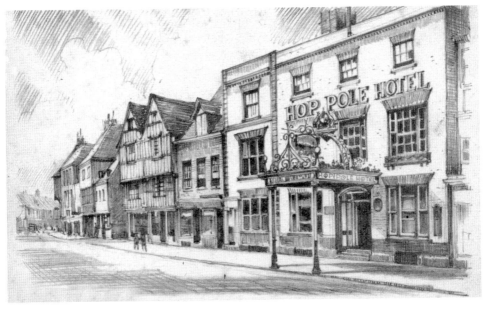

Writing *The Pickwick Papers* Dickens drew deeply on his experiences as a reporter, using the places he knew and, in particular, the inns he had visited. This shows the Hop Pole in Tewkesbury. Dickens wrote, 'At the Hop Pole at Tewkesbury they stopped to dine, upon which occasion there was more bottled ale with some more Madeira and some Port besides, and here the case bottle was replenished for the fourth time. Under the influence of these combined stimulants Mr Pickwick and Mr Allen fell fast asleep for thirty miles.' Many of the people who bought *Pickwick* could recognise the Hop Pole. Those who did not could imagine.

John Forster, lawyer, editor and writer, who became Dickens's closest friend and business advisor after the novelist had difficulties over the manuscript of *Sketches by Boz*. The friendship lasted all Dickens's life, even though the irascible and pompous Forster sometimes drove him to distraction. Forster was given an unpublished private account of Dickens's life by the writer and knew more about the man than anyone living. He later wrote the first Dickens biography, using Dickens's earlier account as a basis of fact.

Dickens as a young man, at the beginning of his career. Long hair—which he sometimes brushed at the dining table, much to the disgust of more delicate beings—and foppish clothes, he is still the dandy of his youth, enjoying the trappings of success. Small in stature, he was nevertheless striking in appearance and was careful to keep up his immaculate appearance at all times.

All his life Dickens loved wayside inns and public houses, viewing them as places of warmth and safety after the rigours of the road—a hangover from his reporting days when he would often arrive at the sanctuary of the inn wet to the skin and frozen, eager for a pork chop and a bed for the night. This shows one of those favoured inns, the little known Sun Hotel in Canterbury where he placed not just David Copperfield, Mr Dick and his aunt but also Mr Micawber who put up in a small room 'strongly flavoured with tobacco smoke.'

Yet another inn where Dickens stayed, the Saracen's Head in Towcester. Despite the caption to the postcard *The Pickwick Papers* was not written here. He may well have had ideas and thoughts about his future book while staying at the inn but the writing of it came somewhat later in his life. Like so many of the public houses and inns Dickens knew and visited, the Saracen's Head is still there and for years traded on the Dickens connection.

William Makepeace Thackeray

The homes of Literary Men.

Young Street.

Sydney Carter.

With critical and financial success assured, Dickens joined the Garrick Club and became friendly with many of the leading literary and artistic figures of the day, men like Harrison Ainsworth, Daniel Maclise and the actor W. C. Macready. William Makepeace Thackeray, also a member, was a gruff and rather taciturn individual. He and Dickens knew each other quite well—indeed, Thackeray had been considered as an illustrator for *The Pickwick Papers* after the suicide of Robert Seymour—but they never became close friends. There was a degree of rivalry between them but Thackeray knew that he could never match the popularity of Dickens. Even his *magnum opus Vanity Fair* sold, at best 5,000 copies a month, compared with five or six times more for any of Dickens's books.

Women's fashions in the 1840s. The dresses were designed to emphasise the remoteness and mystery of women. They were creatures to be kept at arm's length—not hard to do in exotic and voluminous creations like this. Kate, her sisters and the other women in Dickens's life would have been sorely hampered by such garb in their day-to-day activities. It would have been exhausting and draining to wear such clothes—small wonder women were affected by 'the vapours.'

Thomas Carlyle, one of Dickens's acquaintances. Carlyle was notoriously argumentative and quick tempered. His wife Jane was not much better—someone once said 'Thank God Carlyle married Mrs Carlyle, thereby making just two people unhappy instead of four.' Carlyle looked in askance at some of Dickens's antics—like his acting enterprises—but never doubted his friend's ability as a writer. Dickens, for his part, used Carlyle's monumental history of the French Revolution to inform him of the background when he came to write *A Tale of Two Cities*, claiming to have read the book twenty times.

With *Pickwick* approaching the end of its run, Dickens—acutely conscious of remaining in the public eye—began to write another monthly serial. This was *Oliver Twist*, the story appearing in *Bentley's Miscellany* with the aim of exposing the dens of vice and crime around Seven Dials and also of attacking the despised new Poor Law. One of the central characters was the Jewish fence and criminal Fagin who has enough ambiguity about his character to retain at least some sympathy from the reader. The setting for the story is wonderfully drawn. Dickens was writing about an area he knew well but even so, to maintain two popular serials like this was no mean achievement.

An illustration by the artist Kyd, showing Fagin in his den. The portrayal of the Jewish fence and gang master drew accusations of Anti-Semitism, common enough even at this time, although there is no evidence that Dickens ever harboured or even supported such racist opinions. Conscious of the criticism, however, it was something Dickens later sought to put right in his portrayal of Riah, the kindly and supportive Jew in *Our Mutual Friend*.

The real villain of *Oliver Twist* is the monstrous Bill Sykes. Fagin and the Artful Dodger have at least some redeeming features, Sykes has none. He is a bully of the worst sort, the type of character Dickens must have seen many times in his wanderings around the East End of the city. His murder of Nancy, unconvincing and flat as she might be as a character, demands retribution—which duly happens on the rooftops of London.

Even as he was writing Pickwick and *Oliver Twist* Dickens was considering a new book. In January 1838 he and his illustrator Hablot Browne journeyed to Yorkshire to research that county's boarding schools. These were not really schools at all but places where unwanted children, many of them illegitimate, could be safely sent and forgotten about. Dickens and Browne went to Bowes Academy where the infamous one-eyed William Shaw kept a school—he refused them admission—and looked at other establishments, equally as hideous, in places like Barnard Castle where children had been blinded or even killed. Dickens went away satisfied. He had found his next book and its location, Dotheboys Hall.

Nicholas Nickleby ran alongside Pickwick until the earlier book was completed and then it took over, Dickens thereby completing the amazing trick of writing three serials at the same time, at least for a short while. The character of Wackford Squeers was clearly based on William Shaw but Dickens was not content just to expose the Yorkshire schools. He wrote also about his first love, the theatre, including a warm portrayal of the Crummles family, and took a revengeful pot at his mother—he had never forgotten that she 'was warm' for him to be sent back to the Blacking Factory—in the character of the silly, even stupid, Mrs Nickleby. Introduced almost as an after-thought, Mrs Squeers became, at once, one of the most popular and most hated characters in the book—this postcard view shows her ladling out brimstone and treacle to the unfortunate inmates of the school at Dotheboys Hall.

Wackford Squeers waits for more new pupils at the Saracen's Head Inn—unsuspecting newcomers are brought before him by relatives who want simply to pass on their charges as quickly as possible. An illustration by Phiz for *Nicholas Nickleby*, the drawing perfectly catches the awfulness of Squeers and his regime at Dotheboys Hall. Small wonder the reading public loved the story, delighting in Nicholas's thrashing of Squeers and, at the last, seeing Mrs Squeers force fed the brimstone and treacle she had so often used on the boys.

By the late 1830s the railway boom had really begun to take hold in Britain, new railway lines beginning to cut swathes through the British countryside and whole sections of cities like London being destroyed to make way for the terminus stations. Dickens was an avid admirer and incessant user of the new railways, riding them whenever possible. Always restless, always eager for the next experience, it was the perfect mode of transport for him.

The success of *Nicholas Nickleby*—outselling even *Pickwick*—caused Chapman & Hall to make a gift of £1,500 to Dickens and, more importantly, paying him to edit a new magazine, *Household Words*. The idea was to use the work of other writers as well as Dickens but when people realised that there was not always going to be a serial from the pen of Boz, sales slumped. Dickens's response was, in the fourth issue of the magazine, to begin a new serial, *The Old Curiosity Shop*.

Now seen as overly sentimental and trite, the story of *The Old Curiosity Shop* concerns Little Nell—surely Mary Hogarth in disguise—and her attempts to get her grandfather out of the clutches of the villainous dwarf Daniel Quilp. The story has to be read in the context of the time, however, and the public loved the tale. Dickens himself found the plot's inevitable progress towards the death of Nell incredibly moving and traumatic. He was often in tears as he wrote and the public was certainly in tears as they read. The Irish MP Daniel O'Connell read her death scene in a railway carriage—he hurled the book out of the window, crying 'He should not have killed her!' Even the imperturbable Thomas Carlyle was quite overcome. Letters from readers poured in, begging Dickens to spare Little Nell—all in vain; Dickens knew the value of a good dose of pathos when he saw it and he was not going to let an opportunity like this desert him, no matter how much he was hurting inside and dreaming of Mary Hogarth.

Several houses and shops have claimed to be the original of the Old Curiosity Shop. This postcard shows the inside of one such place. It has no actual connection with Dickens or his novel but it certainly sold many cards to tourists and Dickens enthusiasts who were convinced they had found the true location of the shop where Nell and her grandfather lived. Little Nell became one of his best loved creations and the apocryphal tale of crowds lining the New York quay sides as the boat carrying the latest instalment came in to dock, screaming, 'Is Nell dead yet?' might have a degree of truth about it.

For some time Dickens had been planning a novel about the Gordon Riots, anti Catholic unrest that occurred in the 1780s, but for a variety of reasons the book had never got off the ground. When *The Old Curiosity Shop* finished its run, he decided that now was the time to write the story of *Barnaby Rudge*. It is a tale of mass panic and mob violence in the city and in Essex and although Barnaby, the main character, fails to ignite, the book does have perhaps the best female character he had created to date, Dolly Vardon.

Barnaby's pet bird had its origins in Dickens's own pet, a raven by the name of Grip that lived in the house at Doughty Street and was a great friend of Dickens and his family. Sadly, the bird died but it has been immortalized in Dickens's book, certainly seeming a lot more real and animated than its simple minded owner. *Barnaby Rudge* was one of two historical novels that Dickens wrote. The other was *A Tale of Two Cities*. Neither of them was his best work although the later book was immensely popular.

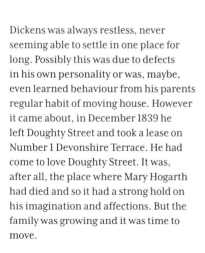

Dickens was always restless, never seeming able to settle in one place for long. Possibly this was due to defects in his own personality or was, maybe, even learned behaviour from his parents regular habit of moving house. However it came about, in December 1839 he left Doughty Street and took a lease on Number 1 Devonshire Terrace. He had come to love Doughty Street. It was, after all, the place where Mary Hogarth had died and so it had a strong hold on his imagination and affections. But the family was growing and it was time to move.

The new house soon began to impose its presence on Dickens and the array of family and friends who visited regularly. Dickens and his family lived for twelve years at Devonshire Terrace in what was a substantial and imposing house with a library, several bedrooms and sitting rooms, grooms quarters, room for servants, cellars and a good large garden where the children—and there were, by now, several of them—could play safely.

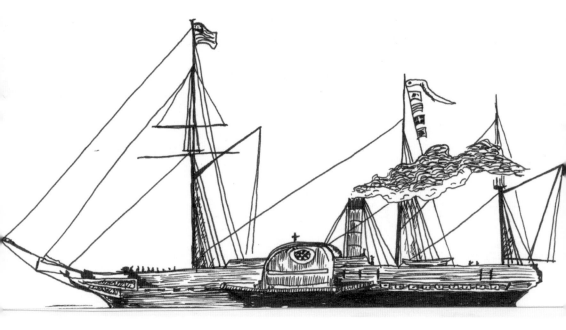

Dickens's stories, in particular *The Old Curiosity Shop*, had long been very popular in the USA and when he received an invitation from the writer Washington Irving to visit America it was almost inevitable that he would agree to go. Leaving their children Charley, Mamie, Katie and Walter in the care of their friend Macready and Fred Dickens—shades of Dickens's own childhood abandonment—in January 1842 Dickens and Kate set sail from Liverpool on the SS *Britannia* the Cunard Line's first steam driven vessel. Dickens was excited at the prospect of seeing a new world while Kate, barely consoled by a painting of the children, was miserable from the beginning—they did not know what they had let themselves in for.

The voyage was horrendous, the worst gales for years battering the SS *Britannia*. Everyone on board, even the sailors, were seasick, although Dickens kept a brave face, trying his best to entertain and amuse his fellow passengers. When they landed in America they were immediately besieged by wellwishers and people eager to get a glimpse of the famous Boz. Wherever they went, from New York to Boston and back again, there was no respite, no privacy, and the enthusiasm of the Americans quickly palled as far as Dickens was concerned. It was not all one-way traffic. When he made unfavourable comments about slavery—still legal in the USA—he was criticised; when he complained about the lack of any copyright agreement that enabled American publishers to pirate his books he was vilified. It was not long before both Charles and Kate were heartily sick of the country.

There was some respite when Dickens and Kate took a trip down the Ohio River on the paddle steamer *Messenger*. Yet even here he was appalled and almost overcome by the Americans' constant use of chewing tobacco and the jets of phlegm that were aimed—often inaccurately—at the spittoons that littered the deck. The Americans considered him 'not quite a gentleman'—Dickens thought even less of them. The scenery was unedifying and he considered the Mississippi River 'a slimy monster, hideous to behold.' The much-vaunted new development of Cairo at the conference of the Mississippi and the Ohio was nothing more than a swamp.

It was not all bad. Dickens did enjoy visiting the American jails and lunatic asylums—although his tendency to prognosticate about the treatment of the inmates only brought him yet more scorn and abuse. The Land of the Free, he decided, this was certainly not. In Washington he met President John Tyler and moved on to make friends with writers like Washington Irving and, in particular, the poet Longfellow and the unknown horror writer Edgar Allan Poe. He was impressed by Niagara Falls but, then, Canada lay just across the river and that was nearly England.

Home beckoned at last and Dickens and Kate crossed gratefully into Canada. They stayed at Francso Rasco's Hotel in Montreal where they were allowed peace and far more freedom of movement than they had experienced in America. At the invitation of the Earl of Mulgrave, a senior officer in the British garrison, and a man who had travelled out to the USA with them on the 'Britannia,' Dickens organised some amateur theatricals, the first time he had taken to the stage in years. Even Kate took a part. Perhaps it was relief. Dickens was as officious and demanding as ever—'I am not,' he said, 'placarded as a stage manager for nothing.' He was the perfect despot but it worked. The plays were a huge success. Then it was back on the boat—a sailing ship this time—and home to Devonshire Terrace and the children.

Dickens's immediate response to the American experience was to write a travel book, *American Notes*. It was a slim and fairly insubstantial offering that really relied on the Dickens name to make its mark. The book appeared in the summer of 1842 and sold well enough, even though American readers disliked it intensely. A much more substantial piece of writing, *The Life and Adventures of Martin Chuzzlewit*, was beckoning, however, and if the Americans had disliked *American Notes* they would hate this one with a vengeance. The story began to appear from Chapman & Hall in early 1843.

The American scenes, occupying barely a quarter of the book, were soon at the forefront of everyone's mind. Dickens established Martin as an architect in his version of Cairo on the Mississippi, a desolate wasteland of mud and swamp—in effect a massive confidence trick. And, of course, it infuriated the Americans. These days the book is read mainly for the two magnificent creations of Mr Pecksniff and Sairey Gamp, but when it was first published it was the American section that caught the public imagination. As might be expected, it brought a huge backlash from the American readers. Dickens did not care, they didn't pay for his books anyway.

The Season's Greetings.

Mrs. Gamp.

Sairey Gamp, the midwife who liked a little drop of toddy and was not averse to imbibing it whenever she could, quickly achieved popularity that equalled that of Sam Weller and Dolly Vardon. Her name was soon appropriated as the slang term for an umbrella, something that has persisted until the present day. And yet, despite the success of Mrs Gamp the book did not sell as well as author and publishers had hoped. Some inappropriate and rather hasty words of criticism from Chapman & Hall put the ever-prickly Dickens on his dignity. How dare anyone criticise his work, he thought and promptly parted company from the publishers who had been instrumental in establishing him at the forefront of English novel writing.

An unusual painting of Dickens dating from around the time of his American trip, showing him with a moustache and the beginnings of a goatee beard. Facial hair soon became a natural part of Dickens's persona—it hid his face, hid his emotions, and like all successful Victorian gentlemen a full beard and side whiskers denoted a powerful and important individual.

Dickens and his family had always taken regularly taken holidays. It began with a cottage at Chalk in Kent where Charles and Kate spent their honeymoon and quickly went on to include trips to the Pleasure Gardens at Cremorne or down river by boat to Greenwich. The family's favourite holiday destination, however, was Broadstairs. Dickens described it like this—'The ocean lies winking in the sunlight like a drowsy lion.' Broadstairs was far enough away from London to be a true holiday destination but close enough to allow the ever-restless Dickens the chance to flee back home whenever he felt the need. Bleak House in this photograph has no connection with Dickens's book of the same name.

Dickens House in Broadstairs. Contrary to popular belief, this was not where Dickens and his family stayed whilst in Broadstairs. A woman by the name of Mary Strong—said to be the original of Betsy Trotwood—lived here and, like Betsy, hated the donkey riders who passed in front of her house on a regular basis. In *David Copperfield* Dickens transferred the house to Dover, a town he did not know particularly well. He knew this house, however, passing it on his regular walks each summer.

Anxious to cash in on his role as the master of popular sentiment, just before the Christmas period of 1843 Dickens brought out what has probably remained his most famous book, *A Christmas Carol*. In it he encapsulated the feeling of Christmas and created, in the old miser Scrooge, one of the most memorable characters in fiction. The three Christmas spirits remain a masterpiece of invention, the ghost story catching the reader and holding him right to the end. It would not be stretching too fine a point to say that, beginning with this book, Dickens created modern Christmas. Certainly it confirmed him as the 'poet' of the hearth and home, the man who, through his popular sentiments, had literally defined the Victorian Age.

By the standards of his other publications *A Christmas Carol* was a small, thin volume but Dickens had gone to great lengths to make sure the book would look attractive when sitting on the book stalls or on people's shelves. Each page had gilt edging and the title was daubed in gold, both on the front and on the spine. Unfortunately, all of this put up the cost of production so that although 6,000 copies were sold on publication day, and critics like Thackeray called it 'a national benefit,' the book failed to make Dickens the profit he desired and expected. It was his last effort for Chapman & Hall, at least for many years, and although he had made the arrangements for the look and style of the book, they took most of the blame for its poor financial showing. With all of his phenomenal success it is hard to envisage Dickens ever being short of cash but he was burdened with a family that made continual demands on his finances—from his mother and father to his siblings and his own children—and, as a young man, he had made several unwise investments. Now he realised he must reduce his spending.

He would, Dickens decided, take his family to Italy—where living was cheap, he had heard—for a year. The journey was long and arduous, the family travelling by coach and river steamer. He had hoped to stay in Byron's old house but it was too dilapidated and in September 1844 the family moved into the Palazzo Peschiere (the Palace of the Fishponds) outside Genoa for the princely sum of £5 a week. The constant ringing of the town's church bells was an irritant to Dickens until he realised they could also be an inspiration. His second Christmas book, *The Chimes*, was directly inspired by these bells. 'The Chimes' was intended to be a fierce attack on the generally held view that poverty was self-induced and that the poor of the land were simply born bad. He was always proud of his books but, when it came out, even Dickens was forced to conclude that he had succeeded admirably in his aim.

November 1844, Dickens reading *The Chimes* to an assembled group of friends that included Forster, Maclise, his brother Fred and Thomas Carlyle. He had made a rapid journey back to London—leaving his family in Genoa—to see the book through the press and took the opportunity to reduce his audience of friends to tears, not only by the power of his words but also his style of reading. Even the normally imperturbable Carlyle was visibly moved. It was a point Dickens noted and put away in the back of his mind for use in the future. Then it was back to Italy for Christmas and a ten-week tour of the country.

A Happy New Year

New Year's day, the best and happiest day-in the whole year, and one that is almost sure to bring Good Fortune with it.

The Chimes
Charles Dickens

Trotty Veck and his daughter Meg.

The Chimes is barely read these days but at the time of its publication it was hugely popular and sold well. Centred on New Year's Day rather than Christmas, the book told the story of little Trotty Veck and his daughter Meg but was really a plea for fair treatment of the poor and reflected a growing awareness in Dickens of the state of the underclass in England. He had already addressed these issues in books like *Oliver Twist* but from this point on he became more active in his help and aid for the needy.

Anton Mesmer, the founding father of the school of mesmerism. Dickens had always been interested in the occult, regularly putting on magic shows for his children and friends. He first heard about Mesmer while in the USA and, soon, discovered that he had the power to mesmerize Kate. In Italy he became friendly with Emile De la Rue and his wife, a woman who suffered from nervous tics and hallucinations. Dickens began a course of prolonged treatment and the De la Rues went with the family on their tour of Italy. Kate was not pleased as most of Madame De La Rue's attacks seemed to happen around midnight and consequently Charles spent several hours away from the marital bed! She was distant with the De La Rues and Dickens tried to disguise the cause of her annoyance. When he was finally forced to tell the truth it probably marked the beginning of the fatal coldness between Charles and Kate.

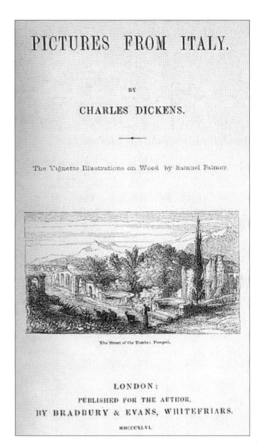

Pictures From Italy was published in 1846, on Dickens's return to England. He used letters he had sent to friends to form the basis of the book and recounted his adventures in Rome, Naples and on Mount Vesuvius—where he climbed to the lip of the crater and returned with his clothes smoldering from the heat of the volcano. The book was one of his best non-fiction works, comments on the urban desolation of the country making it particularly poignant.

Back in England Dickens threw himself eagerly into amateur dramatics, the proceeds going towards charity, and became ever more interested in helping those less fortunate than himself. In November 1847, along with Angela Burdett-Coutts, he was instrumental in the opening of Urania Cottage, a home for 'fallen women.' Dickens drew up the house rules and even interviewed prospective candidates.

All his life Dickens loved to take long walks, particularly at night. It was the one sure way of easing the restlessness than cursed him throughout adulthood. He was particularly fond of the riverside areas of London and knew Wapping Police Station well. The police officers knew him, too, and were overjoyed when he later introduced the station into his book *Our Mutual Friend* as the place where the body of the supposed John Harmon is brought.

Crime had always interested Dickens, his pictures of villains like Bill Sykes and Fagin being some of his most powerful creations. He did not glamorize crime but saw criminals as the manifestation of an uncaring and neglectful society. In a society that had no state support for needy individuals people were bound to turn to crime. In later years Dickens regularly accompanied policemen on their rounds and in his final two books, *Our Mutual Friend* and *The Mystery of Edwin Drood*, was clearly moving towards the genre of detective fiction.

Fiercely opposed to public execution—he had himself once witnessed such a spectacle and been utterly revolted by it—Dickens believed in the reforming nature of prison rather than the punitive one. He wrote many letters to the press on the subject, once declaring that of all the many hundreds currently waiting execution only three had not 'been spectators of executions.' Fear of the gallows, he concluded, rarely prevented the act of murder.

A Board School after education had become compulsory—in the very year that Dickens died. His belief in the power of education was strong—after all, had not the Christmas Spirit once told Scrooge that ignorance was the greatest of all evils? Dickens paid for all his children to attend school—apart from Charley who was sent to Eton at the expense of Miss Coutts. Dickens was appropriately grateful but it is hard to say how Charley felt.

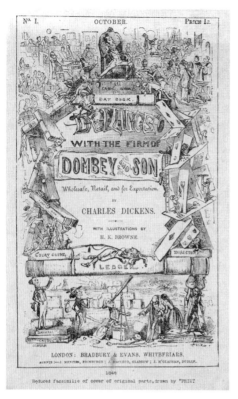

The front cover of *Dombey and Son*, the first of Dickens's 'dark' books. It was begun when the family was on holiday in Switzerland in June 1846 and, to begin with, was not an easy book to write, perhaps because Dickens missed the stimulus of smoky London. He had to lay it aside to write the year's Christmas book—a slight and overly sentimental thing called *The Battle of Life*—but was soon back at the pages of Dombey, the words finally beginning to pour out as the story and the characters took a hold on his imagination.

A sentimental postcard showing Florence Dombey and her doomed brother Paul. Dickens had moved his family to Paris when he wrote the death scene of Paul Dombey, an episode that left him as heartbroken as the death of Little Nell many years earlier. The death of children became a staple part of Victorian poetry and fiction, partly as a result of Dickens's works. Many music hall ballads from the late nineteenth century dealt with infant mortality, partly as a warning, partly as a lesson that whatever is quickly gained can be just as quickly lost. So many of Dickens's fictional children, from Nell and Paul Dombey to little Johnny in *Our Mutual Friend* perished before adulthood that it is hard not to relate such events to Dickens's own virtual 'death' when he was sent to the Blacking Factory as a helpless twelve year old and, inevitably, to his loss of Mary Hogarth.

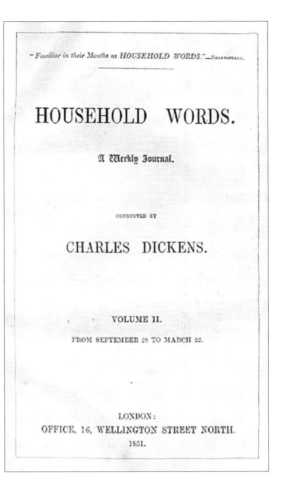

Above left: *Dombey and Son* was an immediate success when the first part appeared in October 1846, selling more than 30,000 copies. Dombey continued to sell well throughout its run, thanks to characters like Captain Cuttle who provided the sombre text with a little humour and lightness. The success of the book finally gave Dickens the financial security he craved and moved his art onto an altogether grander and more serious level. It was a contemporary story, brilliantly capturing the changes that were then affecting Britain, in particular the effect of the new railways on cities like London—'The first shock of a great earthquake had, just at that period, rent the whole neighbourhood to its centre.'

Above right: The front cover of *Household Words*. Dickens edited this monthly magazine for Bradbury and Evans from 30 March 1850 until he quarrelled with the publishers in 1862. It was filled with good quality fiction, the first serial being by the popular Mrs Elizabeth Gaskell, as well as journalism from Dickens. The magazine gave him a platform from which he could attack, with traditional reforming zeal, all of the injustices he saw in society. The magazine was popular, particularly when its main feature was a story by Dickens.

In the autumn of 1848 Dickens's sister Fanny had died and his mind was now preoccupied with images of childhood. Previously he had already written a piece of autobiography, far too personal for publication, and discussed with Forster the possibility of a novel that was based on and around his real life experiences. When he came to write *David Copperfield*—the initials for his hero, DC, are his own reversed, CD—he could not set the story in his childhood environment. That would have been too painful. And so he set the beginnings of the story between Yarmouth and Lowestoft. Blunderstone, a fictional village and rectory based on a real village called Blundeston, might have been the birthplace of Copperfield but it was certainly not the birthplace of Charles Dickens.

Many believe that *David Copperfield* is Dickens's greatest work. Told in the first person, the book is memorable for a whole range of characters, not least the odious and 'ever so humble' Uriah Heep whose unmasking and fall from grace still manage to evoke a happy sigh from most readers. The story appeared in monthly parts in *Household Words* between May 1849 and November 1850 and, while clearly a work of fiction, the reality of so many characters and situations lies only skin deep beneath the surface of the prose.

CHARACTERS from CHARLES DICKENS.

"MR. MICAWBER."
(David Copperfield)

I am, however delighted to add that I have now an immediate prospect of something turning up.

Kyd.

from Victoria

Wishing you a happy

The grand and glorious invention that was Mr Micawber was, of course, John Dickens. With his constant refrain 'I have now an immediate prospect of something turning up,' he has all of the unrealistic dreams of divine providence stepping in to help him—just like Dickens's father. Like John Dickens, Micawber would be plunged into the depths of gloom whenever the family was threatened by creditors but within half an hour he would have put the trouble behind him and be out on the street, visiting all his usual haunts as if nothing had ever upset him, a gentleman to the bone. Mrs Micawber has something of Elizabeth Dickens about her, too, and David's youthful job at Murdsone and Grinby's is directly related to Dickens's own incarceration at Warren's Blacking Factory.

Tavistock House on Tavistock Square, the house to which Dickens moved in 1851 and where he lived for ten years. The lease on Devonshire Terrace expired in November 1851 and Dickens, who had grown inordinately fond of the place, viewed a change of dwelling with trepidation. This was a year of endings and change as Dickens's ninth child, the baby Dora, died in infancy, leaving both Kate and Dickens heartbroken. Before that there had been even greater grief. John Dickens had died after a harrowing operation. But then Dickens found something to take his mind off the grief. He discovered the ideal place to live, Tavistock House, close to the British Museum. By the end of November he and his family had moved in and Dickens's mind began to turn to a story he was planning. It grumbled and rumbled in his belly and became *Bleak House*.

Georgina Hogarth in the 1850s. Kate's young sister Georgina had joined the Dickens household in 1842, when she was just fifteen years old, a family pattern you might say. She was a companion to Kate—and Dickens, too— and acted as a governess to the Dickens children. It was Georgina who taught them to read and write and became devoted, not only to the children but to the master of the house as well. She accompanied the family on holidays to France and Switzerland and was with them during their time in Italy.

The years 1849 and 1850 were ones of amateur dramatics for Dickens, in particular acting at great country houses. In 1848, holidaying with his family in Switzerland, he had met the Honourable Richard and Mrs Watson who lived at the palatial Rockingham Castle in Northamptonshire. At their invitation, Dickens visited the Castle many times, playing charades and acting out small performances as after-dinner entertainment. When the Watson's suggested something more substantial he immediately agreed and brought a large company of amateur actors to the Castle to perform in the Great Hall. The Castle also became Chesney Wold, the home of Lady Dedlock in *Bleak House*.

The homes of Literary Men.
Knebworth House.

Bulwer Litton

The writer Bulwer Lytton had inherited his stately home, Knebworth House, from his aristocratic mother. When he suggested a festival of drama at Knebworth Dickens agreed enthusiastically. Kate Dickens was to have taken a small part in one of the plays but, in keeping with what Dickens called her clumsy self, she fell through a trapdoor during rehearsals, sprained her ankle and had to retire from the role. Rather more successfully, Georgina did take part and Dickens was supposedly so impressive in his various parts that one of the carpenters declared that 'it was a great loss to the public when you took to writing books!'

Dickens intended *Bleak House*, which began its run in November 1851, to be an attack on a wide number of institutions and evils that beset Victorian Britain. These ranged from the Courts of Chancery to poor housing in the city, from poverty and crime to diseases such as cholera and smallpox. This illustration shows the churchyard at Russell Court—'a hemmed in churchyard, pestiferous and obscene'—and is where the book's heroine, Esther, discovers the body of her mother Lady Dedlock. Fog pervades the book, the fog of old London town and the fog of the law, the fog of deceit and the fog of long-standing and misplaced hopes and ambitions.

'Bleak House' is memorable for a range of characters although Esther, the main protagonist—like so many of Dickens's female leads—fails to spark and remains little more than a cypher throughout the book. The lawyer Tulkinghorn and the crossing sweeper Jo are memorable but Mr Turveydrop, a fairly minor character who was 'not like youth, he was not like age, he was not like anything in the world but a model of deportment,' steals the scene whenever he appears. The book is also memorable for the appearance of Detective Bucket, who arrests an innocent man before eventually finding the real culprit. He is Dickens's first detective character.

In February 1855 Dickens was sorting through the morning mail when, with a sudden lurch of the heart, he recognised familiar handwriting on one of the letters. It was from Maria Beadnell, the girl who had so captivated him when he was eighteen years old. Dickens, unhappy in his home life, was determined to keep the renewed contact and would not believe she was other than the girl he had loved and lost twenty-five years before. Despite Maria protesting that she was now 'toothless, fat, old and ugly,' Dickens would have none of it. He must see her again—he was desperate to see her again. And, inevitably she turned out to be exactly what she said. Worse than that, she was also now a simpering, foolish, giggling matron. When Maria and her husband came for dinner it was like having his world smashed away—for the second time. He revenged his damaged emotions in the only way he knew how—he put her, as Flora Finching, into *Little Dorrit*, a masterpiece of caricature but cruel, certainly cruel.

Dickens's unhappiness in his home life and, in particular his marital situation, was kept hidden from all but his closest friends and associates, men like John Forster, his new friend Wilkie Collins and his editorial colleague on *Household Words*, William Henry Wills. He took to roaming the streets more and more, usually by night, his restless spirit and the constant hankering after the one moment, the one experience he had not had, forcing him onwards. The grim reality of his later books owes more than a little to these nocturnal wanderings.

William Dorrit and his daughter Amy finally leave the Marshalsea Prison, an illustration by Phiz. Dickens was obsessed, maybe even possessed, by *Little Dorrit*. The story of old William Dorrit, the father of the Marshalsea, brought back far too many memories of childhood and his father's imprisonment for debt. After *Bleak House* and *Hard Times* it is Dickens's third dark book. And the unhappiness of the author is clear in many of the pages. It was not just his personal situation, he was also deeply unhappy about the state of the country and the disastrous management of the Crimean War, perhaps the most unfortunate and badly run conflict Britain had ever endured. He wrote about it in *Household Words* but his anger and discontent were best seen, far more subliminally, in *Little Dorrit*.

Some measure of relief now came from the pen of Wilkie Collins. Dickens's new friend had written a story, a melodrama called *The Frozen Deep*, based loosely on the doomed Arctic exploration of John Franklin, lost while trying to discover the North West Passage. Together, they decided to stage the play. Dickens worked at the text and then produced it—as well as playing the leading role, a man who dies in the arms of his beloved. It was a perfect way for the arch sentimentalist to lift his battered spirits.

The house at Gad's Hill where Dickens lived for the final years of his life. Dickens and his father had often seen it when the author was still young. He had admired it then, John telling him that if he worked hard he might, one day, own such a place, and when he and his colleague Wills walked past the place in the summer of 1855 his admiration was rekindled. So when, a few days later, his friend Wills learned that the place was for sale he rushed to Dickens with the news. It was as if fate had willed him to own the house. Naturally, Dickens bought Gad's Hill Place, the first house he had ever actually owned. Alterations were quickly made and by February 1857 it was ready for occupation.

Dickens loved Gad's Hill Place, it fulfilled a promise he had made, to himself and his father, to work hard and achieve. He also loved the magnificent cedar trees that graced the estate. Planted by William Brooker of Higham in 1786, they were fully grown when Dickens took up occupation. Unfortunately their condition gradually became more and more dangerous and in 1907, long after Dickens's death, they were cut down. Souvenirs were made from the wood and sold by Dickens Mementoes of Rochester.

Such is Dickens's fame as a novelist that we forget he was also a highly skilled journalist, writing on a range of topics from prison reform to child poverty. When the *Royal Charter* was wrecked on Tuesday 25 October 1859 over 450 people, passengers and crew, were drowned or smashed to pieces on the rocks of Point Lynas on Anglesey. Many of them were gold prospectors from Australia, their newly acquired wealth stashed into their pockets when they were thrown onto the shore. The local vicar wrote hundreds of consoling messages and ministered to the dead and dying. Dickens visited the area soon afterwards to meet the vicar and record his impressions and feelings about the disaster. He wrote, 'Here, with weeping and wailing in every room of his house, my companion worked alone for hours, solemnly surrounded by eyes that could not see him, and by lips that could not speak to him, patiently examining the tattered clothing, cutting off buttons, hair, marks from linen, anything that might lead to subsequent identification.'

There is a cruel irony in the fact that just when Dickens had found the perfect place to live, his marriage and relationship with Kate finally reached breaking point. They had been unhappy, both of them, for a long time. Kate had grown corpulent and indolent—hardly surprising considering the ten children Dickens had inflicted on her—and seems to have suffered from permanent post-natal depression. Dickens, self-obsessed as ever, failed to notice her unhappiness—or at least do anything about it. There were times he could hardly bear to look at her. As he later wrote to Forster, 'We are strangely ill-assorted for the bond there is between us. God knows, she would have been a thousand times happier if she had married another kind of man.'

Matters came to a head in 1857 when Dickens received a request to put on his production of Collins's *The Frozen Deep* at the Free Trade Hall in Manchester. The play had already been performed before Queen Victoria and Prince Albert and such a request took Dickens's mind away from his unhappy home life. For such a performance, however, amateur actresses would not do—professionals were required. Frances Ternan and her two daughters Maria and Ellen were recommended to Dickens. Maria played the heroine, opposite Dickens, but it was the youngest of the Ternan girls, eighteen-year-old Ellen, who captured Dickens's imagination. More than that, she captured his heart and he fell, wildly and without reason, for this girl who was the same age as his own daughter Katey.

Ellen was not a great actress and she was certainly not a conventional beauty. There was a hard edge to her, something remote and calculating that she seems to have used to her advantage in her dealings with Dickens. She might have been calculating but to Dickens she represented the innocence and vitality of youth, the very qualities he was beginning to lose sight of in himself. He longed to be free to do as he wished and Ellen, it seemed, was waiting there, almost within touch, almost obtainable—but he had to be rid of his wife first.

Dickens had already withdrawn from the marital bed but when a bracelet intended for Ellen was sent, by mistake, to Kate she was furious. She challenged him and Dickens, immediately defensive, upbraided her for casting aspersions on such a young and innocent creature as Ellen. His remarks were hardly fair, even though, at this stage, his relationship with Ellen was probably still platonic—due more to Ellen's reluctance than Dickens's—but he went one stage further. Kate, he declared, must show the world that there was nothing untoward going on by paying Ellen a visit. Katey Dickens, hearing her mother sobbing, declared that she should not go. But Kate did not have the strength or the will to oppose her husband and the visit was duly made.

When rumours of his relationship with Ellen began to circulate in society Dickens, now almost beside himself with longing and anger, decided to issue a public denial. John Forster tried to prevent what was a personal matter becoming public but Dickens insisted and published a rebuttal of the rumours and stories in *Household Words*. Other papers also carried the short article or letter. Thackeray had never been close to Dickens but one day, entering the Garrick Club, he heard other members—alerted now to the scandal, thanks to Dickens's letter—declaring that the affair was between Dickens and his sister-in-law, Georgina Hogarth. 'No, no,' Thackeray declared. 'It's with an actress.' Dickens heard about the comment and was outraged. The two men did not speak again until 1863 when, at Thackeray's instigation, they finally shook hands. Dickens's anger knew no bounds and when he heard of derogatory comments made about himself and Ellen by the Hogarth family he forced them to retract their comments, publicly—on pain of Catherine being abandoned and cut off with nothing. Dickens then moved into a small apartment at the *Household Words* office while the intricate problems of a legal separation were conducted and Kate was set up in a house of her own in Camden Town.

The blame for the marriage breakup was easily and cleverly thrown on Kate, about whom Dickens wrote, 'In the manly consideration towards Mrs Dickens which I owe my wife, I will merely remark that the peculiarity of her character has thrown all the children on someone else.' The 'someone else' was her sister Georgina, who continued to live in Gad's Hill, to act as housekeeper and bring up the youngest children, Harry and Plorn. Dickens and Ellen continued their affair, almost certainly not sexual, at least not for several years. She cleverly managed to keep him at a distance and many people believe that she was actually repulsed by the thought of sexual relations with him. His patronage and his generosity, fair enough; his physical attentions—not until it was absolutely necessary. Whatever she felt, it was inevitable that she would eventually give in and although the actual date of her 'surrender' remains more than a little unclear, it probably happened in the mid-1860s.

For years Dickens had enjoyed the mantle of champion of the family, house and home. He was the master of popular sentiment, lauding domesticity and the value of a good, mutually beneficial marriage. That epithet had been rudely and publicly broken. And yet, strangely, the breakup of his marriage had virtually no effect on his popularity as a writer. Of course there could be no question of a divorce from Catherine—that, certainly, would have been disastrous both for his reputation and for the sales of his books.

Contrary to popular belief Dickens did not use just one illustrator for his books, although the famous Phiz clearly remains the best known. Over the course of his long career artists as varied as Luke Fildes, George Cruikshank and R. W. Buss all illustrated his work. This postcard view shows Marcus Stone who drew the illustrations—far more 'photographic' or realistic than the drawings of Phiz—for *Our Mutual Friend* and, if Dickens had lived, would have gone on to work on many more of his books.

MR. CHARLES DICKENS'S LAST READING.

Above left: Dickens at his reading desk in front of his adoring public. By the late 1850s Dickens was being subjected to numerous calls for financial aid. As well as supporting Kate, his nine surviving children, his widowed mother and several of his brothers and their wives, he was now also actively supporting the three Ternan women. He needed to earn money and when a public reading he gave to raise funds for the Great Ormond Street Hospital proved to be phenomenally successful, he was clear—public readings would raise him the money he required. John Forster was dismayed, thinking it undignified and ungentlemanly, but Dickens—as in all things when he had set his mind—was insistent. In August 1858 he began a reading tour that took him from Plymouth to Edinburgh, via Ireland, and provided him with a huge sum of money in return, certainly far more than he could earn from writing. When he saw the profit even Forster was forced to admit that Dickens had been right although, from this early stage, he became increasingly concerned about the effect the readings were having on his friend's health.

Above right: Mr Weller, the elder, by Kyd. *Pickwick Papers* was, from the beginning, one of the most popular of all Dickens's readings. The audience laughed and cried as he took his place behind the specially constructed reading desk and, literally, became Pickwick, Tony Weller or Sergeant Buzfuz. Mrs Gamp from *Martin Chuzzlewit* was always popular with audiences and, of course, an adapted version of *A Christmas Carol*. Dickens had a six-man entourage accompanying him on his reading tours around Britain, including a gas man—crucially important in the days before electric lights—a valet and Albert Smith, his first tour manager.

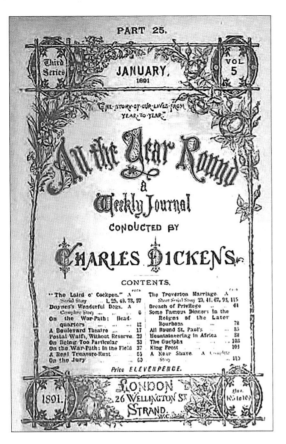

PART 25.

Third Series

JANUARY, 1891

VOL 5

THE STORY OF OUR LIVES FROM YEAR TO YEAR

All the Year Round

a Weekly Journal

CONDUCTED BY

CHARLES DICKENS

CONTENTS.

LONDON
26 WELLINGTON ST STRAND. W.C.

1891.

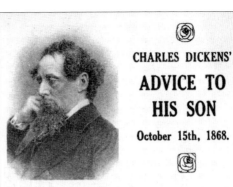

CHARLES DICKENS' ADVICE TO HIS SON

October 15th, 1868.

WHATEVER you do, keep out of debt and confide in me. If you ever find yourself on the verge of any perplexity or difficulty, come to me. You will never find me hard while you are manly and truthful.

As your brothers have gone away, one by one, I have written to each of them what I am now going to write to you. You know that you have never been hampered with religious forms of restraint, and that with mere unmeaning forms I have no sympathy. But I most strongly and affectionately impress upon you the priceless value of the New Testament, and the study of that book as the one unfailing guide in life. Deeply respecting it, and bowing down before the character of our Saviour, as separated from the vain constructions and inventions of men, you cannot go very far wrong, and will always preserve at heart a true spirit of veneration and humility. Similarly I impress upon you the habit of saying a Christian Prayer every night and morning.

These things have stood me all my life, and remember that I tried to render the New Testament intelligible to you, and lovable by you when you were a mere baby—and so God bless you.

Ever your affectionate Father,

October 15th, 1868   CHARLES DICKENS.

Above left: The cover of Dickens's periodical *All the Year Round* which he began to edit in 1860. Dickens's publishers, Bradbury & Evans, had refused to publish his 'Personal Statement' concerning Kate and Ellen. He immediately broke with them, returning to his original publishers Chapman & Hall. It meant that *Household Words* was finished but Dickens still needed a publicity machine and he immediately suggested a new weekly magazine, *All the Year Round*. Chapman & Hall were happy to print and circulate the magazine. It was an instant success but his anger at Bradbury & Evans remained—when his eldest son Charley married the daughter of Evans, Dickens refused to attend the wedding.

Above right: A postcard with Dickens's advice to one of his sons. Dickens's sons were a disappointment. When they were young he could fuss them, give them bizarre nicknames like Chickenstalker and The Ocean Spectre. It was only as they grew up that they and Dickens grew apart. Charley was declared bankrupt in 1868, Walter died in India and left many debts, Francis returned from the Bengal Mounted Police and repeatedly insulted the family. Sydney joined the navy but was such a spendthrift that he was forbidden to even visit. Edward Bulwar Lytton, the youngest—Plorn as he was known—lived a life of debt and hardship in Australia. Only Alfred and Henry were in any way successful, Alfred as a farmer in Australia and Henry as a barrister who earned a knighthood.

Dickens in the garden at Gad's Hill, reading to his daughters Katey and Mamie. Katey, called 'Lucifer Box' by Dickens, was a fiery personality who took her mother's side in the marriage breakup. Shortly afterwards she married the weak and ineffective Charles Collins, brother of Wilkie. 'But for me,' he was supposed to have wept, 'Katey would not have left home.' Mamie never married and became her father's constant companion during the last ten or twelve years of his life.

The Swiss Chalet in amongst the cedars at Gad's Hill. Given to Dickens by the French actor Charles Fechter—a frequent visitor to Gad's Hill—the chalet came in fifty-eight boxes and was put together like an early version of Lego. It was given to Dickens as a way of thanking him for a gift of £3,000, given to Fechter to save him financial embarrassment. Dickens used the upper room as a study and often wrote there in the summer—'My room is up amongst the trees,' he said, 'and the birds and the butterflies fly in and out.' The chalet and Gad's Hill itself became, increasingly, a place of refuge for Dickens.

Visitors to Gad's Hill Place were encouraged. They were entertained with highly organised and hard fought cricket matches and long walks in the countryside around Rochester and Chatham, often with one or other of the dogs that Dickens, in his role of 'country squire,' now kept. One visitor who was not particularly welcome, however, was the Danish fantasy and fairy tale writer Hans Christian Anderson who came in 1857 and stayed for over a month. He was a bore who knew virtually no English and found it difficult to communicate with his hosts. When he finally returned to Denmark, Dickens put a card in his room—'Hans Christian Anderson slept in this room for five weeks which seemed to the family ages.'

A regular port of call on the long walks which Dickens took around the Gad's Hill area—both on his own and with guests—was the Leather Bottle Inn at Cobham. The inn had featured in *The Pickwick Papers*, being the place where Mr Tupman had sought refuge after he was jilted by Rachel Wardle. As Mr Pickwick declared, 'this is one of the prettiest and most desirable places of residence I ever met with.' Like so many of the inns and public houses mentioned in one or other of Dickens's books, the Leather Bottle traded unashamedly on his name for many years.

After the success of *A Tale of Two Cities* Dickens intended to take a break from writing. But the new serial by Charles Lever, which began in *All the Year Round* at the end of 1860, did not attract the interest of readers and Dickens saw no alternative but to run a story of his own alongside Lever's. It was called *Great Expectations* and was probably the most complete and perfect story he ever wrote. Told in the first person, the story concerns young Philip Pirrip (Pip) and, clearly drawing on his memories of childhood on the Kent marshes, begins with an encounter with an escapee from the prison hulk moored just off shore. It is a chilling and memorable scene, the nightmare fear of young Pip reaching out to each and every reader.

Cooling Church, shown here at night, when shadows would have flickered across the gravestones and the imagination of someone like Dickens would have run riot. This was the spot where Pip first met Magwitch and passed on much needed food and sustenance. Dickens's compassion for the escaped convict more than over-reaches Pip's fear, making the opening chapters of *Great Expectations* one of the greatest pieces of writing in the English language.

The implausibility of Miss Haversham and her life dedicated to self-pity is more than compensated for by the quality of the writing. This postcard view shows Restoration House in Rochester, the model for Miss Haversham's Satis House. It is a grim place, full of dust and mold, reflecting the grimness of the opening scenes of the book. On the day before his death Dickens visited the place again, probably intending to use it once more in one of the scenes in his new book, *The Mystery of Edwin Drood*.

A portrait view of Bulwar Lytton who persuaded Dickens to change the original ending of *Great Expectations*, with Pip left a solitary man, his dreams of a life with Estella unfulfilled, to a happy conclusion when she has a sudden change of heart. Happy ending it might be, realistic it is not. Apart from the love story of Pip and Estella, convicts and the threat of ruin dominate *Great Expectations*. Dickens was drawing on his memories when the men on the convict ships in the Medway, waiting for transportation to Australia, would come shore to work in the dockyard, 'numbers on their backs, as if they were street doors.'

Dickens, family and friends in the garden at Gad's Hill Place a year or so before his death. Left to right, Charles Dickens Jnr, Katey Dickens, Dickens, Miss Hogarth, Mamie Dickens, Wilkie Collins and Georgina Hogarth. The saddest element of the picture is the missing wife, the spectre at the feast. And not even Ellen Ternan there to keep him happy! Dickens may have got his way but it is hard to see him as a contented man in the final years of his life.

By the 1850s, railway travel had become the most effective and most efficient way of moving around the country. Dickens, always eager for new experiences, gladly embraced this new mode of transport. It is hard to see how he could have managed his reading tours, endlessly circling Britain, leaping onto trains for his next destination as soon as each performance finished, without the use of railways. Railways come into several of his stories, both with unscrupulous investors and incidents such as the death of the villain Carker. His short story 'The Signalman,' part of the 'Mugsby Junction' series, is actually set in a railway signal box.

Dickens, a portrait photograph taken in the late 1860s. Here it is easy to see the lines of premature age on his face while the receding hairline is in complete contrast to the youthful and luxuriant locks of the 1830s and '40s. The beard was no affectation—as well as being 'in fashion' it helped to hide the lines and signs of tiredness. There is no doubt that he drove himself too far, too fast. Had he slowed down to take things just a little easier, he might have had another ten or twenty years of life. But that would not have been Dickens's way.

Dickens's penultimate novel, *Our Mutual Friend*, was dominated by the River Thames which runs like a menacing thread throughout the pages. The river brings wealth but it is also a harbinger of death and misfortune. The story appeared in *All the Year Round* between April 1864 and November 1865 and each number was written well in advance—at least to begin with. The more the book progressed, the more Dickens slowed down with his copy. He was in poor health and the writing did not come easily.

Rogue Riderhood, one of the most interesting characters from *Our Mutual Friend*. The publishers, Chapman & Hall, were eager for a successful outcome to this new story and, as a consequence, the book was advertised everywhere, on the sides of omnibuses and at railway stations. But it failed to catch the imagination of the public, sales dropping from an initial 35,000 to just under 20,000. Now *Our Mutual Friend* is seen as one of the greatest of his books, the start of a new direction and power to his fiction. But that was not how it was viewed at the time.

Jenny Wren, the disabled dolls' dressmaker, strikes perhaps the only discordant note in the book, particularly when set against characters like Mr Boffin, the Golden Dustman, and Bella Wilfer. She is a typical Dickens female character, all sentiment and effete goodness. She stands in complete contrast to Bella Wilfer who is probably the best and most realistic of all Dickensian heroines—with more than a little of Ellen Ternan in her. She talks like a real person and, offered the choice of money or marriage to a poor man, chooses love and what she supposes will be poverty. Mr Riah, the good and honourable old Jew, was deliberately put in to disarm critics who were still complaining about the picture of Fagin in *Oliver Twist*. Like Jenny Wren he is not a totally convincing character and lacks much of the vitality of Fagin.

Mr Podsnap from *Our Mutual Friend*. The character was based quite deliberately, and very accurately, on John Forster, Dickens's long time friend. By the mid 1860s the friendship between the two men had cooled slightly—thanks to the Ellen Ternan affair and the growing importance of Wilkie Collins in Dickens's life—and Dickens was happy to give Podsnap many of Forster's pompous mannerisms. Forster failed to notice the similarities, in particular his habit of rendering anything unpalatable or undesirable as non-existent. As Podsnap says, 'I don't want to know about it; I don't choose to discuss it; I don't admit it.' Forster probably looked at Dickens's lampooning of him in the same way.

The public readings continued, Dickens's schedule being carefully monitored by his new manager George Dolby, a man who Mark Twain was later to call, 'A gladsome gorilla.' One evening at Birmingham a badly placed gas jet almost burned through the wire holding a glass reflector above Dickens's head. Dolby was terrified and signed his master to come off to safety but Dickens read on calmly until he reached the end of his paragraph and then left the stage. By now, despite Dolby's ministrations, the readings were taking a terrible toll on Dickens's nervous and physical health. He was affected by neuralgia and gout in his right foot was so bad that he could barely pull on his boot.

On Friday 9 June 1865 Dickens, Ellen and her mother were returning from a short break in Paris when their train was involved in a major accident. Just outside Staplehurst in Kent the engine hit a section of track that had been removed by workmen and not replaced. No warning signs or signals had been erected. The train was derailed on a viaduct, the carriages plunging into a field and many passengers were killed and injured. Dickens's carriage was left hanging precariously above the field, one of the few not to plummet down twenty or thirty feet. Dickens and his women managed to escape injury in the crash, although they were badly thrown about. He comforted them and then helped the two Ternan's to crawl out to safety.

A contemporary drawing of Dickens at the Staplehurst Disaster. After the crash Dickens courageously and caringly helped many of the injured passengers, giving them water—and brandy— from his hat. Then he suddenly remembered that the manuscript of *Our Mutual Friend* was still in the carriage and he climbed back in to retrieve it. The accident caused Dickens considerable stress, what we would now call post-traumatic shock and, arguably, he never recovered from it. His health began to deteriorate ever more quickly and he could never again sit easily, without emotion, on a railway train—although he continued to use them, right up to his death.

Dickens in 1868, the year he finally returned to America. For several years Dickens had been asked to make a visit to the USA to give some of his famous readings. He knew that it would be financially advantageous but he was wary after his last experience at the hands of the Americans. In 1867 George Dolby was sent out to the New World discuss a possible reading tour. He reported back quite favourably. The Americans had largely forgotten the furore of *Martin Chuzzlewit* and *American Notes* some twenty-five years before and were now anxious to hear him read. And so, in 1868 Dickens sailed for Boston and, despite his fears, it was clear from the start that his privacy would be respected by the American public. The readings were an unmitigated success. Dickens journeyed to New York and Washington—where President Andrew Johnson brought a party to hear him read every night for a week.

Despite arranging another reading tour for the autumn, this time what was termed a farewell tour in England, Dickens's mind was now turning to a new novel. And here, at the end of his life, he returned to his beginnings in Kent. *The Mystery of Edwin Drood* was to be set largely in Rochester (which he called Cloisterham) although several scenes were also located in the opium dens of East London. By now, however, the scenes of high humour and joviality about Rochester which are to be found in 'Pickwick' had been replaced by a more sombre and disquieting tone. Cloisterham/Rochester was, he said 'a drowsy city—a city of another time and a bygone time—with its hoarse cathedral bell, its hoarse rooks hovering about the cathedral tower'.

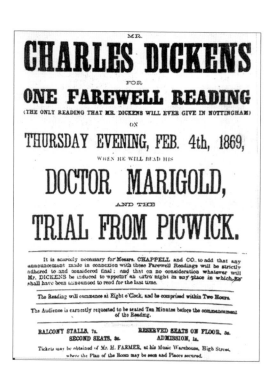

The first number of 'Drood' appeared in April 1870 and by then Dickens's final reading tour had been underway for some months. He was finding it increasingly difficult to cope with the strain of nightly readings and writing the new book but he could not give up—he loved to feel the audience (for his books and for his readings) in the palm of his hand—the old actor was not dead yet. He had been forbidden to read in April 1869, doctors fearing for his life, but was soon on the podium once more, the doctors agreeing that he could read but only in London in order to keep the travelling down to a minimum. This poster from 1869 advertises readings from *Pickwick* and *Dr Marigold*, a perennial favourite with audiences.

Jasper Drood declares his love for Rosa Budd, an illustration by Luke Fildes of Dickens's final book, *The Mystery of Edwin Drood*. Jasper, the wicked uncle of young Edwin and the drug-addicted choirmaster of the cathedral at Cloisterham, is the villain of the story and the most interesting of all Dickens's final characters. Dickens left no hint at where the story would have gone, had he been able to finish it, although Forster did declare that Dickens had intended Jasper to be the murderer, with the last chapter being written in the condemned cell. Dickens also apparently instructed Fildes to draw Jasper with a double neck tie as this was the implement with which he was going to strangle Edwin. Yet Dickens was the master of the 'red herring' and the truth, now, will never be known.

Jasper's Gatehouse in Rochester, at the entrance to the Cathedral Close. Whether Jasper did actually murder Edwin will never be known. In his previous book, *Our Mutual Friend*, Dickens had supposedly killed off John Harmon, only to bring him back from the dead at the end. The idea of re-birth attracted Dickens—after all, was that not what the affair with Ellen Ternan was really all about? So, perhaps, Edwin was due to return and expose his would-be murderer? It is all part of the delicious mystery that surrounds this last book.

Another Fildes illustration from *Edwin Drood*. Perhaps under the influence of Wilkie Collins, author of *The Moonstone* and *The Woman in White*, perhaps as the inevitable progression of his own fascination with crime and criminals, Dickens was clearly in the process of inventing a new genre, the detective story, at the moment of his death. It would have been fascinating to see where his interests took him had he been allowed only a few more years.

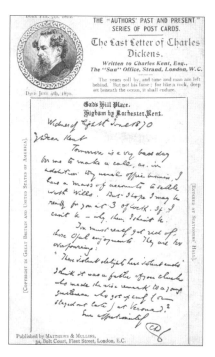

A postcard showing the last letter ever written by Charles Dickens. Dating from the day before his death, the writing is scrawled and untidy, as if Dickens was aware he did not have long left. He had already given his last reading on 15 March 1870 at St James's Hall in London, commenting, 'from these garish lights I vanish now for evermore with one heartfelt, grateful, respectful and affectionate farewell.'

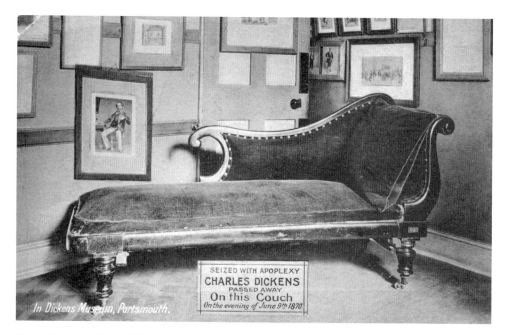

SEIZED WITH APOPLEXY CHARLES DICKENS PASSED AWAY On this Couch On the evening of June 9th 1870

In Dickens Museum, Portsmouth.

The end came on 9 June 1870, five years to the day after the Staplehurst Disaster. All that summer he had been in relative retirement at Gad's Hill, working on *Edwin Drood* and finding time to be presented to Queen Victoria. On 8 June he came down from the Chalet where he had been working and sat for dinner with Georgina. It was clear he was unwell. He suddenly pushed back his chair, stood up and said that he had to go to London, then he collapsed. He was carried by servants to the dining room sofa and a doctor was summoned, but it was hopeless. He had suffered a major paralytic stroke and it was clear there would be no recovery. Charley, his daughters and Ellen were summoned and duly arrived during the evening.

The empty chair, Dickens's study at Gad's Hill—not in the Chalet but in the main house. All through the night of 8/9 June Dickens lay on the couch, breathing laboriously and watched over by the four women in his life. Finally, just after six o'clock on the following evening, his breathing became shallow. A tear rolled down his cheek and he died. He was just fifty-eight years old and *The Mystery of Edwin Drood* was not even half completed. In his will Dickens left £1,000 to Ellen Ternan and the bulk of his property and money to his family. His real legacy, however, rests in his words, the glorious tales he told and the characters he created. His stories and characters have been abidingly popular all over the world, particularly in countries like America, Italy and France.

The interior of Westminster Abbey. Dickens had originally wanted to be buried alongside Mary Hogarth but that was clearly not possible. Then he had thought of the churchyard at Shorne. Public opinion, however, demanded more and *The Times* suggested that, as he was such a public figure and his works such a significant benefit to everyone, that he be laid to rest in Westminster Abbey. And so it was in Poets' Corner, five days after his death, that the restless body of Charles Dickens was finally interred. There was no official mourning— something he had dictated in his will—and the memorial stone stated only his name and dates of birth and death.

SELECT BIBLIOGRAPHY

Ackroyd, Peter, *Dickens*, Sinclair-Stevenson, London, 1990

Amos, William, *The Originals: Who's Who In Fiction*, Sphere, London, 1985

Anon, *Mr Pickwick's Kent,* W. & J. Mackay & Co, London, 1899

Carradice, Phil *Welsh Shipwrecks*, Quotes, Buckingham, 1993

Fitzsimmons, Raymond, *The Charles Dickens Show*, Geoffrey Bles, London, 1970

Greaves, John, *Dickens at Doughty Street*, Elm Tree Books, London, 1975

Hibbert, Christopher, *The Making of Charles Dickens*, Longmans, London, 1967

Green, Frank, *London Homes of Charles Dickens*, Printing Craft Ltd, London, 1928

Hardwick, Michael and Mollie, *Dickens's England*, J. M. Dent & Sons, London, 1970

Johnson, Edgar, *Charles Dickens*, Penguin, London, 1986

Kaplan, Fred, *Dickens: A Biography*, Hodder & Stoughton, London, 1988

Langton, Robert, *The Childhood and Youth of Dickens*, Hutchinson, London, 1891

Philip, Neil & Neuburg, Victor (Eds), *Charles Dickens: A December Vision*, Collins, London, 1986

Priestley, J. B. *Victoria's Heyday*, Book Club Associates, London, 1974

Slater, Michael, *Dickens and Women*, J. M. Dent & Sons, London, 1986

Tomalin, Claire, *The Invisible Woman*, Penguin, London, 1991

Tomalin, Claire, *Charles Dickens: A Life*, Penguin, London, 2011

Watts, Alan S. *The Life and Times of Charles Dickens*, Studio Editions, London, 1991